# The Dyslexia Handbook 2011

Edited by **Bernadette McLean** and **Geraldine Price**
Managing Editors **Rachel Lawson** and **Debbie Mitchell**

Published by
**The British Dyslexia Association**
Unit 8, Bracknell Beeches, Old Bracknell Lane,
Bracknell, RG12 7BW

Helpline: 0845 251 9002
Administration: 0845 251 9003
Website: www.bdadyslexia.org.uk

**Front Cover designer:** *Flags and sun: Whitstable 2010*
Cover artwork, taken from 'The Book Flags' project by Jon Adams, Artist in Residence, Portsmouth University. The aim is for audiences to become the artist and create tens of thousands of flags recycled from book pages woven into a series of outdoor synchronous public artworks. For details of how to create your own 'Field of Flags' and be part of this ongoing project head to **www.dysarticulate.org**

ISBN 978-1-872653-52-5

9 781872 653525

£10.00 (inc P&P)

# The British Dyslexia Association

The British Dyslexia Association aims to ensure that there is a way forward for every dyslexic person so that he or she received appropriate teaching, help and support and is given an equal opportunity to achieve his or her potential.

# The Dyslexia Handbook 2011

A compendium of articles and resources for dyslexic people, their families and the professionals who deal with them.

Edited by **Bernadette McLean** and **Geraldine Price**
Managing Editors **Rachel Lawson** and **Debbie Mitchell**

Published by
The British Dyslexia Association

# Editorial Note

The views expressed in this book are those of the individual contributors and do not necessarily represent the policy of the British Dyslexia Association.

The BDA does not endorse the advertisements included in this publication.

Whilst every effort has been made to ensure the accuracy of information given in this handbook, the BDA cannot accept responsibility for the consequences of any errors or omissions in that information.

In certain articles the masculine pronoun is used purely for the sake of convenience.

British Dyslexia Association

The Dyslexia Handbook 2011

1. Great Britain. Education
2. Bernadette McLean and Geraldine Price
3. ISBN 978-1-872653-52-5

Published in Great Britain 2011 Copyright © British Dyslexia Association 2011

Printed by Information Press, Eynsham, Oxford
**www.informationpress.com**

Advertising sales by Space Marketing
Tel: 01892 677740
Fax: 01892 677743
Email: **brians@spacemarketing.co.uk**

British Dyslexia Association
Unit 8, Bracknell Beeches, Old Bracknell Lane, Bracknell RG12 7BW
Helpline: 0845 251 9002
Administration: 0845 251 9003
Fax: 0845 251 9005

Website: **www.bdadyslexia.org.uk**

BDA is a company limited by guarantee, registered in England No. 1830587
Registered Charity No. 289243

# Contents

# Editors' Introduction

Bernadette McLean Principal HADC
and Geraldine Price University of Southampton

We have had enormous enjoyment editing this handbook; to some extent it has been like holding a party, a celebration for the many contributors who have shared in American brunch style their expertise and experience across a wide range of contexts. We feel that there is something for everyone: be it parent or professional.

For parents, the chapters that they will be drawn to, we suspect, are Choosing a School, How Parents Can Help with Reading and Reasonable Adjustments. Helpful also are the chapters which offer suggestions for training those memory skills (Bark) and the concentration skills (O'Regan) that are often less than efficient in children.

Professionals will be particularly interested in the developments that have taken place over the last year, many stemming from the Rose Review. There is increasing recognition that training is vital for all supporting those with dyslexia, ranging from specialist teacher training to training for Classroom Teachers and Support Assistants. We need to promote recognition and understanding of dyslexia and its impact upon learning for older students. To this end we are pleased to include chapters from Lavington and Bloom. The chapter on supporting art students complements the chapter on music.

Widening contexts are further signposted in the chapters on supporting and assessing dyspraxic and dyscalculic learners.

Teachers need to be able to find and evaluate appropriate teaching resources for students of all ages; it is not a case of one size fits all. We value the contributions therefore from Capener and Reilly who offer alternative approaches at word level literacy teaching because we know that synthetic phonics is not the answer for all learners. Other chapters focused on a learner-centred approach with the metacognitive and affective issues that are considered in the chapters by Price and Amesbury.

In New Insights into the Demography of Dyslexia, Campbell asks some interesting questions about gender and dyslexia and some comments in McNicol's chapter offer a complementary view.

As usual technology has its place to play and two chapters are devoted to IT solutions. As we proceed through the 21st century technological tools are becoming the norm for all people. "Technology is now an embedded part of every young person's learning." Siabi

Two chapters deal with on international perspectives. Paphiti outlines the support system in Cyprus and the progress made in recent years. Reid offers a global view of the development of policy and provision over the last 20 years in countries including the Czech Republic, New Zealand, Canada and Kuwait; he concludes that the situation in the UK "is still rosy in comparison with some other countries".

The Rose Report has triggered discussion about definitions of dyslexia; the BDA definition incorporates that of Rose but takes it one step further by including visual processing difficulties justifying the inclusion of the chapter by Stein. In view of the most recent research into the prevalence of dyslexia in languages such as Japanese, this is to be applauded.

The legacy of the Rose report may be far reaching and the most recently published White Paper (November 2010) outlining a more academic approach to education will present challenges for those learners with processing and memory difficulties.

Nevertheless, the current interest in Every Child Matters is placed in a context of social inclusion chapter and reinforced through the recent CAF (November 2010). It is therefore crucial that the most appropriate and relevant teaching methods are adopted thus the advice in the Muter chapter should be studied by both professional and parents.

We thank the BDA for inviting us to edit this handbook and all those who have contributed to it.

# Introductions

# Dyslexia – the Abominable Snowman

Sir Jim Rose

Some years ago I saw a car sticker in the USA which said in bold print: *'Dyslexics of the world untie'*. Beneath it was written: *'Dyslexia is no joke'*. Not surprisingly, parents of children with dyslexic difficulties often suffer deep anxieties when they perceive that little or no effective support is available to help their child overcome these difficulties.

For many years dyslexia, like the Abominable Snowman, only ever left disputable footprints in the snow. No-one seemed capable of capturing the beast, let alone taming it; arguably, all that has changed. Thanks yet again to Charles Darwin, ably assisted by new technologies and research in cognitive neuroscience; we can now say that some manifestations of dyslexia are heritable. It runs in families and is located on identified genes. In other words, science rather than hearsay tells us that the beast exists.

In consequence, highly respected researchers worldwide have no hesitation in applying the term dyslexia to developmental learning difficulties in reading and spelling. The independent report, 'Identifying and Teaching Children and Young People with Dyslexia and Literacy Difficulties' (Rose 2009) therefore stated:

- Firstly, dyslexia is identifiable as a developmental difficulty of language learning and cognition. In other words, it is now widely accepted that dyslexia exists.

- Secondly, the long-running debate about its existence should give way to building professional expertise in identifying dyslexia and developing effective ways to help learners overcome its effects.

Obviously, responses to dyslexia are shaped by how it is defined so the report stipulated a working definition of dyslexia in keeping with its remit:

- Dyslexia is a learning difficulty that primarily affects the skills involved in accurate and fluent word reading and spelling.

- Characteristic features of dyslexia are difficulties in phonological awareness, verbal memory and verbal processing speed.

- Dyslexia occurs across the range of intellectual abilities.

- It is best thought of as a continuum, not a distinct category and there are no clear cut-off points.

- Co-occurring difficulties may be seen in aspects of language, motor co-ordination, mental calculation, concentration and personal organisation, but these are not, by themselves, markers of dyslexia.

- A good indication of the severity and persistence of dyslexic difficulties can be gained by examining how the individual responds or has responded to well-founded intervention.

Furthermore, because dyslexia can be associated with phonological (speech processing) problems, diagnostic techniques are being developed to identify children at risk of literacy difficulties before reading begins, for example, in nursery provision. Difficult questions remain, such as: *Should all children be screened for dyslexia and if so, how early is it reasonable and reliable to do so?*

That said, debate about issues, such as screening, ought not to stand in the way of making sure that all teachers of beginner readers should at least have a working knowledge of what to look for that indicates a child may be at risk of dyslexia and know where to seek advice on how to provide the best support. For example, all teachers should be able to pick up on the indicators of dyslexia that Hulme and Snowling (1997) have usefully set out for developmental phases from pre-school to adulthood:

| Developmental phase | Signs of dyslexia |
|---|---|
| Preschool | • Delayed or problematic speech<br>• Poor expressive language<br>• Poor rhyming skills<br>• Little interest/difficulty learning letters |
| Early school years | • Poor letter-sound knowledge<br>• Poor phoneme awareness<br>• Poor word attack skills<br>• Idiosyncratic spelling<br>• Problems copying |
| Middle school years | • Slow reading<br>• Poor decoding skills when faced with new words<br>• Phonetic or non-phonetic spelling |
| Adolescence and adulthood | • Poor reading fluency<br>• Slow speed of writing<br>• Poor organisation and expression in work |

We do not yet have answers to all the riddles of dyslexia and how best to counter many of its effects. However, as this handbook shows, remarkable progress is being made such that the prospects for helping far more children to overcome dyslexic difficulties look increasingly promising.

# What is Dyslexia

Dr Kate Saunders

Dyslexia is one of a range of Specific Learning Difficulties (SpLDs). Also included in this umbrella term are:

Attention Deficit Disorder (ADD)/Attention Deficit Hyperactivity Disorder (ADHD) – this condition includes difficulty sustaining attention and ADD can exist with or without hyperactivity.

Dyscalculia – specific difficulty with aspects of mathematics.

Dyspraxia/Developmental Co-ordination Disorder – involving difficulty with motor co-ordination and organising some cognitive skills.

Dysgraphia – difficulty with fine motor skills, especially for handwriting.

Asperger's Syndrome – this includes difficulty with certain interpersonal skills and may be seen as the mild end of the autistic spectrum.

Specific Language Impairment.

The Rose Review (2009), 'Identifying and Teaching Children and Young People with Dyslexia and Literacy Difficulties', commissioned by the government in England provided the following working definition of dyslexia and its characteristics:

'Dyslexia is a learning difficulty that primarily affects the skill involved in accurate and fluent word reading and spelling.

Characteristic features of dyslexia are difficulties in phonological awareness, verbal memory and verbal processing speed.

Dyslexia occurs across the range of intellectual abilities.

It is best thought of as a continuum, not a distinct category and there are no clear cut-off points.

Co-occurring difficulties may be seen in aspects of language, motor co-ordination, mental calculation, concentration and personal organisation, but these are not, by themselves, markers of dyslexia.

A good indication of the severity and persistence of dyslexic difficulties can be gained by examining how the individual responds or has responded to well-founded intervention.

In addition to these characteristics, the BDA acknowledges the visual processing difficulties that some individuals with dyslexia can experience and points out that dyslexic learners can show a combination of abilities and difficulties that affect the learning process. Some also have strengths in other areas such as design, problem solving, creative skills, interactive skills and oral skills.

Some dyslexic individuals experience visual processing difficulties. These can include visual stress, visual tracking problems, binocular visual dysfunction and difficulty with visual-motor perception. They may mis-sequence and reverse letters or numbers, report that letters 'move', lose their place more frequently reading across lines of print, be sensitive to the 'glare' from the white page/board/screen and their eyes can tire more easily when reading. Non-dyslexic individuals can also sometimes suffer visual stress symptoms.

Difficulty with phonological processing is widely accepted to be a key difficulty for many dyslexics. Difficulty linking the letter shapes to letter sounds, breaking words down into sounds, or building strings of sounds up into words and understanding of the way sounds work within words can undermine the early acquisition of written language skills. Sound discrimination, hearing the difference between certain letter sounds, word retrieval and speed of processing can also be problematic for some dyslexic individuals.

Some dyslexic individuals also experience elements of another SpLD. These are referred to as 'co-morbid' or 'co-occurring' difficulties.

# NOT ALL SCHOOLS ARE THE SAME

Not all schools achieved 80% Grades A*-C at GCSE, and 78% Grades A-C at A-level last year.

Not all schools are located in beautiful North Devon, with the River Torridge, stunning surf beaches and dramatic Exmoor and Dartmoor on their doorstep.

Not all schools have their own nationally-famous Dyslexia Centre, with three full time members of staff dedicated to helping each and every pupil to achieve their full potential.

Not all schools ensure that dyslexic students are totally integrated into every aspect of school life, including more than 60 clubs and sporting activities.

Not all schools promise your child a high degree of personal support within a mainstream educational setting in a beautiful part of the country.

Not all schools contain the Grenville Dyslexia Centre.

GCSE RESULTS 50% HIGHER THAN NATIONAL AVERAGE

## KINGSLEY SCHOOL
BIDEFORD

www.kingsleyschoolbideford.co.uk

Dyslexia has a genetic foundation and tends to run in families. It is not always shown in one of the parents (although it often is), but there is generally someone in the wider family (e.g. a grandparent, cousin etc.) who has experienced difficulty with the acquisition of written language skills. In families where dyslexia is present, there can also tend to be a higher proportion of individuals with other Specific Learning Difficulties (not necessarily co-occurring in the dyslexic individuals).

It is clear from research findings that dyslexic brains are not only physically different to non-dyslexic brains, but they also work differently, particularly with regard to processing phonological information and written language. Evidence for structural differences has come from post-mortem research and functional differences can be seen from research involving monitoring brain activity during reading and language-related tasks (e.g. using magnetic reasoning and other neuroscience monitoring techniques).

Research findings have also indicated that the brains of dyslexics can show increased numbers of 'ectopias'. These are clusters of brain cells that disrupt the normal migration of brain cells during pregnancy. This migration process would normally facilitate the development of the language specialisation in the left hemisphere of the brain. Why this happens in dyslexic individuals is not known (there is no known link with any 'environmental' aspect of pregnancy – it just seems to be something that occurs in a certain percentage of the population).

What is clear is that the dyslexic brain makes the early acquisition of language skills more difficult for that individual than for non-dyslexics.

Much more is known now than was known 20 years or so ago about effective teaching for dyslexic individuals (a useful reference is 'What Works for Pupils with Literacy Difficulties: The effectiveness of intervention schemes' by Greg Brooks, now available online – see link on Dyslexia SpLD Trust website **www.interventionsforliteracy.org.uk**). With good dyslexia whole school practices, early identification, effective specialist teaching, intervention (and enough of it) where required together with good monitoring of progress and appropriate adjustments, there is no educational reason these days why the vast majority of dyslexic individuals should not learn at the very least, functional reading, writing and spelling skills. Ideally they should be taught well enough to enable them to fulfill their own potential. Tragically, it is the absence of some of these beneficial conditions that 'causes' the frustration and reduced life prospects of some dyslexic individuals these days, just as much as the underlying dyslexic difficulty itself.

Early identification is crucial as this provides the best long-term prognosis and helps to prevent the secondary emotional, self-esteem and sometimes behavioural difficulties that can otherwise arise. Where there is dyslexia in the wider family it is prudent for individuals and all teachers to be aware of early identification signs. 'At risk' features may be evident from as young as three years of age (please see **www.bdadyslexia.org.uk** for an early identification checklist). Work to build up effective pre-literacy skills (e.g. sound discrimination, visual discrimination, sequencing skills and speech articulation) can help to provide a solid platform for subsequent learning.

From 5–6 years of age, children who show difficulties with the acquisition of early written language skills can benefit greatly from some additional help. It may be appropriate, for example, for them to have a 'booster group' (e.g. a teacher or teaching assistant to pupil ratio of perhaps 1:4) for additional work on phonological skills (i.e. learning the links between letter shapes and sounds and how to build up and break down words into their constituent parts). A multi-sensory approach is advised (e.g. using touch, vision and hearing or saying simultaneously). Wooden or plastic letters can be particularly helpful for some dyslexic individuals for when the message from the eyes may be causing confusion; touching the shape of the letter may give a more secure message to the brain of what that letter shape actually is.

For some children this 'booster group' help (e.g. from Year 1 for perhaps 2–3 terms) will be enough to enable them to 'catch up'. For those who continue to experience difficulties with written language some more targeted and specialist one-to-one help may be required. Specialist dyslexia teachers should be used to help plan and/or deliver the 'booster group' and one-to-one intervention work, monitor the progress of the children and adjust the provision accordingly. An experienced SpLD/Dyslexia-trained teacher or suitably qualified chartered psychologist will also be able to carry out a more detailed diagnostic assessment. An understanding of the profile of the child, including both weaknesses and strengths, can then be used to plan an effective teaching and support programme. Schools should also have access to and use the skills of, a specialist, trained SpLD teacher to ensure that they have effective early identification processes in place, to assist the in-service training from teachers and teaching assistants and ensure that good dyslexia-friendly teaching and classroom environments are taking place in every lesson across all subject areas (please see **www.bdadyslexia.org.uk** for details of Dyslexia-Friendly Schools information). The challenge is 'If they can't learn the way we teach, can we teach the way they learn?' (Harry Chasty, Circa 1987).

Many children's services and schools take part in Dyslexia-Friendly Schools schemes, adopting a 'whole school' approach, building in dyslexia-friendly practice to their policies, teaching and learning, classroom environments and partnerships with parents and pupils. Part of this process includes building the positive self-esteem of dyslexic pupils as well as providing effective intervention work where appropriate.

Teachers that have taken part in the Dyslexia-Friendly Schools process often report that it has encouraged and helped to embed what is good practice, not only for dyslexic pupils, but for the pupils with other special educational needs.

There is much that is good for dyslexic learners in some current classroom well-structured phonics teaching methods. Ways of presenting material that involve the use of active, multi-sensory learning (e.g. using pictures, humorous memory anchors and actions) can help the dyslexic learner. However, the pace of the curriculum can be such that some dyslexic individuals can benefit from more reinforcement to embed learning.

On the positive side, many dyslexic individuals view their dyslexia as a strength as well as a difficulty at times. Some consider that their brains do work differently to those of non-dyslexics and that they are, therefore, able to 'make connections' that others perhaps can not. Strengths in a number of areas have often been noted in dyslexic individuals, including strong creativity, problem solving skills, 3D design ability and verbal communication skills. A higher proportion of successful entrepreneurs are dyslexic than is proportional in the general population.

Successful dyslexics can show huge resilience, hard work and determination (often they have needed these qualities from an early age).

The British Dyslexia Association is a charity that aims to bring about a Dyslexia-Friendly Society, where all dyslexic individuals can fulfil their potential.

### References

Aylward, E.H., Richards, T.L., Beringer, V. W., Nagy, W.E., Field, K.M., Grimme, A.C., Richards, A.L., Thonson, J.B. & Cramer, S.C. (2003) Instructional treatment associated with changes in brain activation in children with dyslexia. *Neurology*, 61, 212 – 219. cited in: *Duncan Milne Teaching the Brain to Read*. (2005), Smart Kids (UK) Ltd. (82)

Brooks, G. (2002) What Works for Pupils with Literacy Difficulties: The effectiveness of intervention schemes, Department for Education and Skills DCFS 00688-2007BKT-EN

Chasty, H. (circa 1987) Dyslexia Action Training Conference.

Fawcett, A.J. (Ed.) (2001) *Dyslexia: Theory and Good Practice.*

London, Whurr publishers.

Hulme, C. & Snowling, M. (1997) *Dyslexia: Biology, Cognition and Intervention.*

Whurr publishers Ltd.

Milne, D. (2005) *Teaching the Brain to Read,* Smart Kids (UK) Ltd.

Reid, R. & Wearmouth, J. (2002*) Dyslexia and Literacy: Theory and Practice.*

John Wiley and Sons Ltd

Rose Review (2009) 'Identifying and Teaching Children and Young People with Dyslexia and Learning Difficulties', DCFS Publications. Download from: **www.teachernet.gov.uk/ publications** Ref: DCSF-00659-2009

Saunders, K. & White, A. (2002) *How dyslexics Learn: Grasping the Nettle.*

Evesham, PATOSS.

For video clips of famous dyslexics: **http://www.xtraordinarypeople.com**

**Patoss**, The Professional Association of Teachers of Students with Specific Learning Difficulties is for all those concerned with the teaching and support of students with SpLD: dyslexia, dyspraxia, ADD and Asperger's syndrome.  Working across all age ranges and in all sectors our members are involved in assessing current levels of knowledge and ability, planning and delivering programmes of work, advising on the broader educational programme, and liaising with other professionals.

**Patoss** aims to promote good practice amongst professionals and has published guidance for teachers, parents and established practitioners. Popular titles are:

*How Dyslexics Learn: Grasping the Nettle* by Saunders and White, helpful and accessible to parents, dyslexics and others interested in the field

*Dyslexia: Assessing for Access Arrangements* by Backhouse et al, published in conjunction with the Joint Council for Qualifications, essential for specialist teachers, heads of centres, governors, exam officers, SENCOs, ALS managers and all those involved in the process

*Dyslexia? Assessing and Reporting* edited by Backhouse and Morris, providing practical guidance for specialist teachers and educational professionals in training, as well as SENCOs and learning support staff working in schools and colleges.

**For further information contact Patoss**
**tel:  01386 712650  email: patoss@sworcs.ac.uk**
**or visit www.patoss-dyslexia.org**

patoss

THE PROFESSIONAL ASSOCIATION
OF TEACHERS OF STUDENTS WITH
SPECIFIC LEARNING DIFFICULTIES

# Parents

# How Parents Can Help with Reading: Laying the Foundations

Patience Thomson

The other day my husband David was caught on camera speeding. That meant three points on his licence or a retraining course. Not surprisingly he chose the latter. I rang to arrange a time and at the end of the call the female voice asked, 'One last question, is your husband dyslexic?' She did not ask, 'Has he mobility problems?', or 'Is he hard of hearing?', but 'Is he dyslexic?' 'Why do you need to know,' I asked. 'Because if he is we must give him more time to read the paperwork and make sure he can follow all the instructions.' I was amazed and thrilled. At last, I thought, dyslexia is becoming recognised and acknowledged in the wider world. This is what we have all hoped and dreamed would happen for so long. Here was not only acknowledgement, but action. Did this herald a new era for dyslexia, I wondered? I brooded on all the areas where help is still so badly needed for the seven or so million illiterate or sub-literate individuals in Britain who struggle with text. What about the supermarkets? Why can't they have a picture of contents on their packaging and clearer print. What about newspapers? Can't they supply a better index and some easier way to navigate around the dense print and highlight the articles of real interest to the individual reader? And what about instructions for all our new gadgets? Have any manuals ever been tested on consumers?

Even in the world of dyslexia, where I have worked for 40 years, many of the books on the subject are not easy to access, with their technical terms, long paragraphs and challenging sentence structures. Just as with teaching in class, the touchstone for textbooks is not 'Is all the information there?', but 'How much is understood and remembered?'

I was commissioned recently by Quick Reads to write a book for parents, '101 Ways to get your Child to Read'. The company

I co-founded some ten years ago, Barrington Stoke, published it. Though it did not say so on the cover or anywhere in the text, this book had a reading age of eight. Parents of children with reading problems are often under-confident readers themselves.

The book had two aims: to impart a better understanding of dyslexia and to offer a wealth of easy practical ideas detailing how parents could help. Anecdotal stories not only helped the reader to memorise the ideas and facts presented, but also suggested that reading about how others had coped was a chance to 'join the club'. Parents could discover that they were not alone and that reading problems were both common and treatable.

Which ideas did the parents find most helpful and which gave them the most to think about? Feedback has been interesting.

Many had not realised that reading was not an isolated problem. The most important point to get over was that reading was often the tip of the iceberg. Problems with expressive and receptive oral language often underlie difficulties with text. Speaking and listening skills are fundamental to the smooth acquisition of reading and writing skills and here parents have a vital role to play, which needs no specialist skills to perform. They can help their child develop a love and understanding of words.

Parents are often juggling these days with a great many different demands and as a result their minds are everywhere at once. They are often not listening properly, especially to their own children. Parents nowadays have less time to devote to reading to their children and families rarely chat together over meal times. Evenings are spent in front of the television or on the computer, which does not foster conversation skills. It is hardly surprising then that children, who soak up attitudes like sponges, are not going to concentrate for long on what others are saying or maintain a logical conversation. This bodes badly for them in the classroom, as so much instruction demands high quality listening skills. Later, when reading a book, they will not be consistently aware of what the author is telling them.

Children also need to hone their expressive language and learn to talk about their ideas, their needs and their emotions in terms that are meaningful and understood. This only comes with practice and the listener must be paying attention and responding. This is part of the parents' essential role. Children need language for communication, comprehension, memory and even thought throughout most of their waking hours.

When a school class starts learning to read, children with a wider vocabulary and a better knowledge of the structure of the English language will have firmer foundations to build on. They will progress faster because they can guess and predict words.

If parents are less likely to read to their children, they are also less likely to be reading much themselves – are there books around the house or is it all manuals, magazines and newspapers? Do the family read aloud together? Do parents model reading? Reading can be an isolating activity for children used to interaction and frequent stimuli. Books read together for enjoyment with a parent, sharing excitement, jokes and a good story take on new attractions. Reading in class can also be fun, especially sharing jokes, but asking children to read to themselves from a book not of their choice as a nightly chore sends out some very negative messages about the purpose of reading.

There comes a time when a child's reading ability has increased to the stage where they are reading 'real' authors and then there may be companionship between author and reader where they are conspiratorially bound together. That is why so many children have cut their reading teeth on series like Enid Blyton's Famous Five. Buying a child several books by the same popular author makes a great deal of sense.

The three great rules are 'Never patronise' with a book that is too childish, it will end in boredom and undermines confidence, 'Never underestimate' how much all children appreciate a good story and 'Never short change' – concentrate on the best and most inspiring and exciting popular books. Reading any old book just for practice is a killer.

Many parents are concerned that it is often the children with reading problems who seem to be lonely in the playground, finding it harder to make friends and join in group discussions. Why should this be? Surely reading is not *that* cool! We come back to the underlying language difficulties. Children struggling to express themselves under pressure will miss out on the body language, facial expression and tone of voice in others and will, therefore, fail to pick up vital social clues.

Parents can do much to enable children to 'read' social situations by identifying and discussing background information. Words are not heard in isolation, they are linked to moods, intentions, attitudes and emotions and conversation must be 'read' in this way.

Parents need to spend prime time with their dyslexic children on an individual basis and to use the opportunity to let them express themselves with no competition and no time pressure. The parent will not be teaching the child in a formal sense but will be exploring vocabulary, honing listening skills and developing confidence in handling language. This will not only have an impact on reading skills but will affect every aspect of the child's life.

If all the parents of the many dyslexic children out there understood dyslexia, its causes and effects, then surely they could be recruited to campaign for better provision for those with language difficulties in many more aspects of life. Their knowledge could be harnessed to promote the sort of awareness that was demonstrated so sympathetically by the traffic police who booked my husband.

# Choosing a School for Your Child

Brendan Wignall

The first thing to note here is that this article is not called 'choosing a school for your dyslexic child'; there is a reason for this. While I will focus later on the issues for parents of dyslexic children it is worth acknowledging at the outset that choosing a school for any child is a potentially fraught exercise for a caring parent and many of the most important factors to consider in choosing a school will be common to all parents.

There is no substitute for a personal visit to the school. In the independent sector this should be a normal part of the admissions process. An open day event will usually be helpful; while such events are often decried on the grounds that they are stage managed by the school (one would be worried if they weren't!), a perceptive parent should easily be able to look past the artifice and gain a feel for the ethos of the school. While a personal visit to a school in the maintained sector may be difficult to arrange in some cases the open/information events should be helpful in gaining an insight into the ethos of the school – which is far more important than shiny new buildings.

Beyond the personal visit and the open day, word of mouth is, of course, useful – but only if it is word of mouth from parents with similar educational values to your own. If you value an education which looks to individual focus and development, a recommendation from a parent on the grounds that a school achieves high results is not likely to be of much relevance.

Mention of high results leads me to consideration of performance tables. Such tables do give information and some of it useful, but not necessarily in the obvious way. In the independent sector, if a school is doing a poor job for the majority of its pupils it will close and a good thing too. Of course that is not the only reason or even the main reason why schools close in the sector. So far as independent schools are concerned, league tables tell you more about the selection policies of a school than anything else. Highly selective schools should score highly in the performance tables, but this does not mean that they are adding any more value than a less selective school of more modest ranking and it is very unlikely to be the case that they focus more on individual pupils than the more averagely ranked school.

The relationship between league table performance and maintained schools takes one into risky and controversial political waters. Undoubtedly there are some poor-performing schools that are in that position because they are poor schools, but continue to operate because the market disciplines that apply to independent schools do not apply in the maintained sector. However, there are plenty of apparently poorly performing schools doing an excellent job for their pupils. Unfortunately, Ofsted judgements cannot be relied upon, so good schools with relatively low examination results may be judged unfairly negatively. Similarly, there are high-performing schools that are not pupil focused and are coasting along because they have a 'good catchment'.

In short, 'objective data' should be treated with great care and a little suspicion. Indeed, to turn the situation on its head, the parents of a dyslexic child – and indeed the parents of any child who would like their son or daughter to be treated as an individual – should be wary of a high-performing school that places excessive emphasis on that high performance. As a parent you should not be interested in how many pupils achieved A* grades at GCSE and A level, or how many got into Oxford or Cambridge. Instead your focus should be upon the school's emphasis – or lack of it – on helping all its pupils to achieve their full potential, whatever that might be. Ideally this desire for achievement should go well beyond the academic.

I believe that my own school does a terrific job for its dyslexic pupils, but that – in part – is because the ethos of the school places individual development and achievement, in all its forms, at the heart of our enterprise. We have a fantastic Support for Learning Department, well accommodated and properly staffed, but good. Specifically focused provision for dyslexic students can only be a necessary foundation, never the solution on its own, to the challenges dyslexic pupils face. Good specialist provision is hugely important, but what goes on in the maths, English and history classrooms, for example, is just as important and – unless it is a specialist school – it is this non-specialist environment in which dyslexic children spend most of their educational lives.

The focus on the non-specialist classes brings us back to the subject of school ethos. When considering a school look at its promotional materials. If they're smart and well presented then well done to the school, but look past the surface appearance; does the school make it clear that it celebrates individual achievement or does it boast about the number of A* grades its pupils achieve? Does the school make it clear that it has a vision of education that goes beyond the classroom, or does it simply make vague mention of an 'after school' activity programme (one suspects this phrase almost always means 'not taken seriously')?

It is impossible to overstate the importance of the ethos of the school for any pupil, but it is particularly important for any pupil with special needs.

Having emphasised the importance of ethos there are some specific questions that can be asked of a school in relation to its dyslexia provision. Is it CReSTeD accredited? If not, why not? Ignorance, a desire not to have 'too many enquiries from dyslexics' and an inability to meet the criteria are all possible answers.

Of those three possibilities, potentially the least worrying is the final answer. A school could be working towards CReSTeD criteria and be heading in the right direction, therefore, worthy of consideration. There is a CReSTeD category suitable for just about every type of school. The other two answers suggest a lack of interest or – worse – an attitude towards dyslexic pupils that suggests that it is worth having a few for the money or the capitation but that too many might get in the way. I wouldn't want my child to be in a school with such an attitude to human beings regardless of whether he or she was dyslexic.

As to specific questions that can be asked I would suggest a look at the CReSTeD website at **www.crested.org.uk**, where there is plenty of advice, including a list of questions taken from Ruth Birnbaum's 'Choosing a School for a Child with Special Needs'. Don't forget the advice about ethos, though; as I have already remarked, the importance of ethos cannot be overstated (which is why I conclude by repeating the point again).

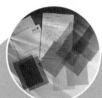

# Reasonable Adjustments

Sue Flohr

More than 10,000 calls came into the British Dyslexia Association's (BDA) Helpline over the past year from worried parents and carers who just did not know where to begin with putting in adjustments to help their child. If you are feeling like this then first check that there are no underlying contributory factors.

It is a good idea to make sure that your child is receptive to learning and that he has no problems with listening or visual skills. If he failed to grasp nursery rhymes, needs instructions repeated or needs to have his full attention attracted before taking in information, then a hearing check is a must for your 'Reasonable Adjustments To Do List'. Children begin to remember the shape of letters and words very early on, so if they cannot recognise a word from one page to another maybe they are not visually developed and questions need to be asked. They should be receptive to learning. If there are barriers like these in the way then it is going to be difficult in a busy classroom and often not easy for the teachers to spot what is going wrong.

So what can you as a parent or carer do? You can learn more about the problems that could be going on:

- Read the BDA's online information sheets on 'Contributory Factors' and 'Eyes and Dyslexia'.

- Discuss any concerns with the class teacher and/or Specialist Educational Needs Co-ordinator (SENCO) at school.

- Make suggestions that might help such as:

  ○ Letting your child sit in direct line with the teacher and away from distractions such as a window

  ○ Photocopies rather than having to copy from the board

- ○ Worksheets printed onto coloured paper to take away glare

- ○ Sans serif fonts to take away the 'wiggly' bits on printed letters.

- See the BDA information sheet on 'Getting Help for your Child'.

- Read the Department for Education's helpful booklet called 'Special Educational Needs (SEN) – A Guide for Parents and Carers'. It explains the process of getting help and support in school.

- Ask the school secretary for a copy of the school's Special Needs Policy and the contact details for the Governor for Special Needs.

- Join a local dyslexia association to keep informed and find support.

If you are still feeling that you have not done enough to put adjustments in place, then support can be given at home:

- Find time to play listening and visual games rather than doing extra school work (see end for list of stockists).

- Make your own games using meaningful examples:

  - ○ For maths concepts use cutting, sticking, measuring.

  - ○ Dartboards for number bonds.

  - ○ Tables squares.

  - ○ Use small whiteboards so that errors can be easily wiped away.

  - ○ Teach the times tables gypsy style using their fingers.

- Help with reading by making it fun – see '101 Ways to Get Your Child to Read' by Patience Thomson.

- Make little coloured acetate rulers to guide and read through, or buy them from Crossbow.

- Use a Reading Pen when really getting stuck but wanting to be independent.

- Don't miss out on what they can't read – join a listening library and follow along with audio books.

- Surreptitiously incorporate the school spelling list with games from 'Wordshark' for example.

- Tap into a handheld spelling device like the Franklin Spellmaster with fun word games.

Sometimes it is difficult to interfere when children reach secondary school but it can hurt when they are left out of group. You need to make sure that you keep up their self-esteem by encouraging them to keep on with activities that they are good at such as acting, painting or sport but not to miss out where they aren't particularly good. There need be no embarrassment when texting or social networking any longer with all the help that is out there:

- Facebook, Twitter and Blogging can all be done just with speech and a little help from Audioboo, a mobile and web platform that effortlessly allows you to record and upload audio for your friends.

- Still stuck and needing instant spellings? Then why not use the free Dragon App on an iPod Touch to see the word magically appear on screen.

- Emails on smartphones with apps for the iPhone like Dragon Dictate can be useful.

For the latest on reasonable adjustments for GCSE and AS level examinations with time and assistive technology allowances, up-to-date information can be found on the Joint Council for Qualifications website. For more about the regulations, standards and examinations Of-Qual are there to help.

Moving on into further education a raft of reasonable adjustments can be put in place to compensate for dyslexic problems. From text reading software to voice recognition programs, smart pens to audio recorders. If you are wondering what might be the best option then you can join the discussion group on our social networks or ask our team of technology experts.

## References

BDA Information sheets available from:
**www.bdadyslexia.org.uk**

Contributory Factors:
**http://www.bdadyslexia.org.uk/about-dyslexia/schools-colleges-and-universities/contributory-factors.html**

Eyes and Dyslexia:
**http://www.bdadyslexia.org.uk/about-dyslexia/further-information/eyes-and-dyslexia.html**

Getting Help for your Child:
**http://www.bdadyslexia.org.uk/about-dyslexia/parents/getting-help-for-your-child.html**

Local Dyslexia Associations:
**http://www.bdadyslexia.org.uk/membership/directories/lda-directory.html**

DFE publication Special Educational Needs (SEN) A Guide for Parents and Carers – ISBN:978-1-84775-226-0
Tel: 0845 60 22260 (quote ref 00639-2008BKT-EN)

## BDA Store

**http://www.bdastore.org.uk/**

The following are available from the BDA Store:

■ Crossbow acetate rulers

■ Wordshark & Numbershark

■ Nessy

■ Reading Pen

- Text to Speech software: ClaroRead/Texthelp Read & Write

- Voice recognition software: Dragon

- iPod Touch

- IPhone

- Livescribe pen

- Audio recorder

## Listening Libraries

Calibre Audio Library
http://www.calibre.org.uk/

Listening Books
http://www.listening-books.org.uk/

## Books and Resources

**Ideas for reading and maths:**
*101 Ways to Get Your Child to Read* by Patience Thompson
*Dealing with Dyscalculia* by Steve Chinn

**Stockists for all books and resources**
The Helen Arkell Shop

http://www.arkellcentre.org.uk/Bookshop/

**SEN Books**
http://www.senbooks.co.uk/

**LDA**
For listening and visual games
http://www.ldalearning.com/default.aspx

**Cambridge House**
For many dyslexia resources
http://www.cambridgehouse-dyslexia.co.uk/

**Joint Council for Qualifications Access Arrangements**
www.jcq.org.uk/

**Of-Qual**
http://www.ofqual.gov.uk/help-and-support

## For Information on Technology

Audioboo: http://audioboo.fm/

Facebook: www.facebook.com/bdadyslexia

Twitter: www.twitter.com/bdadyslexia

Blog: http://bdadyslexia.wordpress.com

**Contact the BDA New Technologies Computer Group**
http://bdatech.org

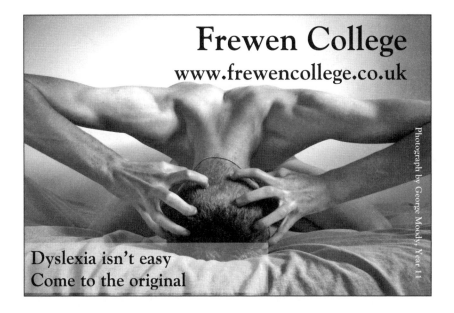

# Teaching Children with Dyslexia – What's Proven and What's Not

Valerie Muter

New treatments for any disorder (be it a medical condition or a learning disorder) tend to attract a lot of media interest and to generate much hope and expectation for those suffering from them. However, for surprisingly many of these treatments, often dramatic claims are made in spite of little in the way of scientific evidence. Dyslexia is not exempt from the claims of the 'miracle cure'. Worried parents and teachers wanting to do the best for their children are often confused by the hundreds of teaching packages and treatment programmes out there, all claiming to be the answer to the child's problems. How do you as a parent choose what is best? Are there criteria that you the teacher can apply to help you decide what teaching materials to buy and use?

This paper aims to guide parents and teachers towards asking the right questions and helping them know how to evaluate the claims made by those promoting dyslexia teaching packages or treatments.

## Questions to Ask of any Treatment or Teaching Package

You've come across a so-called miracle cure for dyslexia which is grabbing headline news or a publisher has just sent out advance information on a new state-of-the-art teaching package. Ask yourself:

1) Is the theory on which it is based scientifically plausible? Does it seem likely that a child's reading skills will improve through balancing on wobble boards or throwing bean bags? Or would it make more sense to use a programme that teaches the child how to connect the sounds they hear in words with how they are represented in print?

2) Is there evidence beyond personal testimonials? Listing quotes from satisfied parents about how their child's confidence has been increased following the teaching programme does not constitute evidence. The 'gold standard' for assessing whether a treatment intervention/ teaching package actually works is the Controlled Randomised Trial (CRT). There are very strict criteria for carrying out CRTs (see Table 1: taken from Bishop 2008). The list may seem daunting but the aims of the CRT are to reduce bias and to eliminate all other possible explanations for observed improvements.

3) Could the alleged improvements made be due to maturation (the child got better as he got older), practice (getting better through repetition) or placebo effects (non-specific or perceived effects of being in treatment)? Carrying out a CRT will get round most of these problems.

4) Have the findings of the intervention study been published in respected peer-reviewed journals? This ensures that other scientists check that the study has been properly conducted before it is allowed to be published in a recognised scientific journal.

5) Are the costs reasonable? Paying a few hundred pounds for a teaching package is acceptable, paying thousands of pounds may not be.

1) Participants must be selected by objective criteria; they should ideally be a fairly homogeneous group (e.g. all poor readers as opposed to having many different sorts of problems) and experience roughly the same degree of difficulty (e.g. falling at least one standard deviation below the mean on a reading test).

2) Participants must be randomly assigned to treatment conditions; they can't self select and there must be no bias as to which condition each participant enters.

3) There must be an appropriate control group which does not receive the treatment; this is essential so you can be reassured that the improvements are due to the treatment and not due to maturation, placebo or practice effects.

4) Pre-treatment test data are essential so we know that all participants are matched at outset (i.e. they start off at the same level).

5) The sample must be a good size; if there are too few participants then the 'statistical power' is inadequate and the results become very difficult to interpret.

6) Assessors must be 'blind' to group status; those carrying out the 'before' and 'after' testing must not know in which treatment group each participant is placed.

7) Trainers or teachers delivering the treatment must not be the assessors, so as to avoid biasing the results in favour of particular groups.

8) The intervention must be clearly described so that it is replicable by other researchers and of course by practitioners too.

9) All data must be reported; it is important that 'inconvenient' findings that don't fit the theory (sometimes called 'outliers') are not excluded without good reason.

10) Statistics used to test differences between the treatment conditions must be appropriate and should quote 'effect sizes' (to show that the differences are clinically and educationally significant and meaningful).

**Table 1: Criteria for Carrying Out Controlled Randomised Trials (CRTs)**

## An Example of a Good CRT

A classic reading intervention study that meets all the criteria for a good CRT was that carried out by Peter Hatcher, Charles Hulme and Andy Ellis in the early 1990s. These authors wanted to demonstrate that teaching poor readers at the *cognitive* level (training up their phonological or 'speech sound' awareness skills) improves their performance at the *behavioural* (reading) level; this seemed to be scientifically plausible, given the huge amount of research evidence demonstrating the connection between children's awareness of the sound structure of words and their ease in learning to read (Question 1). However, the authors strongly suspected that phonological awareness training on its own might not be enough. They hypothesised that the sound training needed to be explicitly linked to the children's experience of print to make it most effective. They began by taking a large sample of 128 poor readers and then randomly allocating them to four different groups (one of them a control group) that were matched for age, ability and reading level; note that these procedures met the CRT criteria 1, 2, 3, 4 and 5. The four groups were: a reading *and* phonology group, phonology alone group, a reading alone group and a control (classroom teaching only) group. All the groups received the same amount of intervention, with the teaching programmes described in detail (criterion 8). The assessors were 'blind' as to which group each child was allocated (criterion 6) and the teachers who delivered the intervention did not assess the children (criterion 7). All data were reported (criterion 9) and appropriate statistical analyses were conducted (criterion 10). These showed that the children making the most progress were those who received the reading *and* phonology programme. The findings were reported in the international peer-reviewed journal Child Development (Question 4). Peter Hatcher went on to develop a commercially available phonological training package called Sound Linkage (published by John Wiley/Blackwell) which is modestly priced (£60) and which has been demonstrated in 'field studies' to help a wide range of children with reading difficulties (Question 5).

## An Example of a Poor CRT

The Hatcher et al. study impressively meets the stringent criteria for carrying out a CRT and the resultant teaching package clearly provides excellent 'value for money'. In contrast, DDAT, a *biological*-based treatment package, claiming to treat not just dyslexia, but also dyspraxia and attention problems, does not. This package is based on the hypothesis that reading problems are caused by motor difficulties that are associated with having an 'underdeveloped cerebellum', a connection which many scientists would regard as theoretically tenuous at best (Question 1). A research trial was carried out by Reynolds, Nicolson and Hambly (2003) which purported to show that children who received DDAT showed a 'three-fold increase in their reading age'. However, the study failed to meet several of the criteria of a good CRT; the sample size of only 35 children was too small and few children had a clear diagnosis of 'reading difficulty' (criteria 5 and 1); there was no comparison of the intervention group's reading ages with those of a control group (criterion 3); the intervention techniques were not described in any depth (criterion 8); and the statistical analyses were often inappropriate, for instance using reading ages when standard scores should have been used (criterion 10). Although the study was reported in the peer-reviewed journal, Dyslexia, it was greeted with a massive amount of criticism on methodological grounds from respected scientists in the dyslexia field (question 4). DDAT is a hugely expensive treatment package (over £2,000) and it is, therefore, doubtful that it addresses the question of achieving 'value for money'.

## Be Healthily Sceptical

It is all too easy to be swayed by interventions or teaching packages that are based on seemingly sophisticated neuroscientific theories, or to be impressed by personal testimonials of miracle cures. The message is, however, to be healthily sceptical and necessarily critical. Looking closely at the scientific evidence for an intervention or teaching package and asking the right questions before you 'buy into it' should help you feel less confused and more confident about the choices you make.

## References

Bishop, D.V.M. (2008) Criteria for evaluating behavioural interventions for neurodevelopmental disorders. *Journal of Paediatrics and Child Health, 44,*520 – 521.

Hatcher, P.J., Hulme, C. & Ellis, A.W. (1994) Ameliorating reading failure by integrating the teaching of reading and phonological skills: *The phonological linkage hypothesis. Child Development, 65,* 41 – 57.

Reynolds, D. Nicolson, R. & Hambly, H. (2003) Evaluation of an exercise-based treatment for children with reading difficulties. *Dyslexia, 9*(1), 48 – 71.

# Teachers and Professionals

# Multi-sensory Learning – The Edith Norrie Letter Case

Jeanne Reilly

The Edith Norrie Letter Case is just as useful now as a **versatile teaching tool** for dyslexics as it was when it was first introduced. In fact, with our increased knowledge of how individuals learn literacy skills and process information the Edith Norrie Letter Case should have a higher profile than it does. It was ahead of its time as a method of teaching spelling.

Essential words to describe the Letter Case today would be: **multi-sensory, auditory, visual, tactile, phonics, phonological awareness, phonetics, alphabetic code, spatial relationship, processing skills, language and meaning**. When Edith Norrie devised her Letter Case the essential words might have been '**word blindness**'.

The original Edith Norrie Letter Case was devised by Edith Norrie herself in her native country Denmark. Already in her twenties and unable to read or spell, she started to work out what we now know to be the key to successfully learning to read and spell – the **alphabetic code**. Each of its teaching principles is carefully thought out so the dyslexic learner can learn and remember letters and sounds for spelling and meaning.

Driven by her wish to read her fiancé's letters she set about working out how sounds were made and created cardboard letters to help her make sense of the written word. Her method helped others who could not read or write. In time she founded the Word-Blind Institute in Copenhagen.

So what does the Edith Norrie Letter Case look like? Practically, it is a box which contains all the letters of the alphabet individually printed on small plastic cards about 1cm wide and 2cm tall. Letters are lower and upper case and are red, green or black. There is more than one of each letter too. There are digraphs; for example, 'sh', as well as essential punctuation, such as speech marks and apostrophes.

| sh |
| --- |

Each letter has its own compartment in the case, gently tilted so all the letters face towards the person using the case. Each letter card is robust enough to be taken out of the case many times and used. Cleverly, the cards have a magnetic back and there is a magnetic board that fits neatly into the case on which to securely place letters being used without fear of them falling on the floor. The newly published Edith Norrie Letter Case uses a clear, simple, modern font that will appeal to all ages using it, as well as the teachers. It can equally be used with primary-aged learners as it can with the older pupils and with adults.

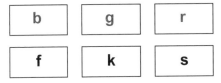

Edith Norrie understood phonetics, **how** sounds are made in the mouth. So she colour coded the letters. The vowels are red, a convention we use today. Green letters represent the sounds using the voice box, e.g. b g r and black letters represent the sounds where the voice box is not used, e.g. f k s.

The vowel cards are in one section of the box for easy access as they are used so frequently. There are also three sections (left to right in the box) which take account of **where** in the mouth the sounds are made – **kinaesthetic** learning. Lip sounds are in the section to the left, for example, b f m. Sounds made by the tip of the tongue are the middle sounds, such as l t. And sounds made by the back of the tongue are to the right, for example, g k. A small plastic mirror as part of the Letter Case, helps the learner to watch his own mouth as he makes the sound, adding another dimension to his learning – visual feedback to support the kinaesthetic aspect along with the auditory information. Multi-sensory learning at its best.

## Teaching Principles

There are 'guidelines' on how to use the Letter Case, with scope for professional judgement. It is an 'aid' or 'tool' to support other materials for spelling.

However, one or two guidelines are worth going over in light of what we know today from research into how dyslexics learn.

1) Introduce each letter slowly, one by one.
   How clever of Edith Norrie to understand that dyslexics are often '**slow processors**'.

2) Make sure the individual understands **how** each sound is made and where in the mouth it is made. Speaking and literacy skills go hand in hand.

3) Learning strong letter sound links is the foundation for learning literacy skills. Spend time on this.
   Edith Norrie understood this many years before it was proved by today's researchers.

4) Edith Norrie worked out many years ago the principles of **phonological awareness** (sounds within words), by promoting contrasts between sounds, voice box versus no voice box and breaking down how sounds were made in the mouth. Speech and language therapists and teachers know that talking and literacy skills go hand in hand.

5) The child must **understand** the words he is learning to spell. After all, learning to spell is a means to an end – a means of enjoying the written word.

6) Moving the letter cards to make words helps the individual understand how words such as hid and hip have different meanings, different sound sequences, as well as different colours for the last letter sound.

# Fulneck School, Leeds

There is no barrier to success

## Independent day & boarding school
## Ages 3-18
## Specialist Learning Support Unit
## CReSTeD registered School

(Council for the Registration of Schools teaching Dyslexic Pupils)

At Fulneck School we aim to identify individual special needs and to provide teaching programmes and strategies to allow all students access to the curriculum at a level commensurate with their intellectual ability.

As a category DU registered School offering a Dyslexia Unit, Fulneck School offers specialist one-to-one tuition within the school as well as support for dyslexic students in all areas of the curriculum.

The pupils can take advantage of individual and small group tuition from experienced specialist teachers, multi-sensory teaching methods and continuity of teaching and support throughout their school career. Our pupils have access to specialist computer software in a dedicated unit to ensure a relaxed, safe and secure learning environment. In-class support is also provided if required.

Contact us today to find out how your child can benefit from a Fulneck School education:

**+44 (0)113 257 0235 or**

**enquiries@fulneckschool.co.uk**

Fulneck School
Pudsey, Leeds
England, LS28 8DS
www.fulneckschool.co.uk
Registered Charity

7) Use the colour-coded letters to show how commonly mispronounced words look on the page, for example, bath, baf. This could help spelling improve, though it might not change how the word is pronounced by the child!

| b | a | th |
|---|---|----|

The Edith Norrie Letter Case is versatile because there are enough letters to make sentences. Punctuation cards can show question marks, speech marks and apostrophes which all add meaning to the written word.

## Considerations when Using the Edith Norrie Letter Case

Be aware that for individuals who are 'colour blind', the red and green letters may look the same colour. There could be another way of distinguishing the vowel cards from the others, a small dot in one of the corners perhaps?

A person with gross or fine motor co-ordination difficulties may find it difficult to handle the small letter cards in and out of the case. However, the teacher can take the letters out of the case and once the letters are on the magnetic board, the learner should be able to push the letters around it to make words and sentences.

The letter cards may not be suitable for the younger dyslexic child to manipulate. They may prefer foam or wooden letters.

Helen Arkell has family links with Denmark. She and Edith Norrie first met in the late 1940s and then in 1953 Helen studied at Edith Norrie's Word-Blind Institute in Copenhagen. The Helen Arkell Dyslexia Centre acquired the rights to publish the Edith Norrie Letter Case in the 1970, translating it from the Danish to English. The Centre is still publishing it today. **www. helenarkelldyslexiacentre.org.uk**

Edith Norrie would not have guessed that her intuitive way of teaching sounds and letters would prove to be spot on in the late twentieth century and is still enduring in the twenty-first century. She would probably have been very pleased however.

# 'From Eggsecqutive to Oesophagus!'

Judy Capener

Throughout the Rose Report there is an emphasis on the most effective method of teaching reading and spelling to the dyslexic learner being through a highly structured systematic 'phonic' approach. Anyone teaching such a learner will know this to be the case. However, there is need for caution as not all the words we need or are likely to need are not 'phonically regular'. There seems to be much of our system of spelling that is not; English being renowned for its lack of transparency!

It also makes the assumption that spelling is primarily the representation of sounds when written words do, in fact, symbolise meaning. Hence, homophones, if not used in the 'write' place, may not upset the spell check tool but certainly will the reader.

'Phonics' is vital for the early stages of literacy development and continues to be necessary for reading unfamiliar words and spelling those not yet in our word banks. However, we should not allow this to be the only level of orthography we teach.

If the dyslexic learner is to avoid the trap of becoming 'stuck in phonics' … as I have been guilty (before I knew better) of allowing my students to write words such as 'filld', 'alsaughts', 'surcul', 'nolledge', 'eggsecqutive' …. they need to understand that there is more to spelling words than relying entirely on how they sound or look.

English orthography (correct spelling) is the combination of three interconnecting systems:

■ Phonology – the sound system of words.

■ Morphology – the structure of meaning within a word.

■ Etymology – the origin of words.

The building blocks of phonology are the phonemes we teach in the early stages of reading and spelling. And it is to this level we return in a phonically based language programme. For many it is the only level of spelling consciously known and understood. However, it is only the beginning of the process of mastering the written word.

Morphology and etymology become increasingly important as our ability to spell increases. Morphemes (the smallest unit of meaning in a word) are given particular attention only as suffixes, prefixes and base/root words. It is unusual for either phonemes or morphemes to be dealt with in terms of their origin. Possibly only learners exposed to the higher level of science vocabulary in their A level studies will be explicitly taught the origin and meaning of parts of words such as the Greek elements of 'methane' 'methyl', 'ethane' and 'ethyl' when they study complex formulae.

Morphology and etymology are the two pieces of the jigsaw we need to add to any 'phonics' programme if we are to give our learners the strategies to become confident, independent readers and spellers.

In order to make sense of how this works it is necessary to know a little about the origins of the English language. Its history explains to a very large extent why the spelling appears awkward and contradictory. For this we have to thank the fact that England is an island which has been much sought after by marauding invaders and finally by conquest.

The 'core' of English is a mix of Germanic languages brought by the Anglo- Saxons and the Vikings. To this was added Norman French following the conquest in 1066 of William of Normandy. This was by nature a language based in Latin, the ancient language of the Romans. The third element is that of Greek which came partly as a result of the proximity of Greece to Rome and later on the rebirth of learning and subsequent research in science, medicine and technology. These languages have kept their structures, idiosyncratic spelling patterns and much of their sense in Modern English.

Etymology is also concerned with meaning but in terms of how words relate to each other as a result of common origins. Take, for example, the words 'here', 'there' and 'where'. These are from Old English, have a similar spelling pattern and base meaning of 'place'. From Latin we have 'inject', 'eject' and 'reject' with the common (what appears to be syllable) 'ject' signifying 'throw'. In these we can see consistency – the parts of the words with the same meanings are usually spelled similarly.

This knowledge is a powerful tool when thinking about the spelling of English as the morphemic structure of words in English and other written languages *OFTEN* determines their spelling.

Structured language 'phonic' programmes do tackle the morphemic level with the introduction of suffixes. They do not, however, always make it clear that this is a distinctly different way of looking at words to a phonemic structure. No reason to worry about whether the suffix 's' has either the voiced 's' or unvoiced sound 'z' – what is vital is knowing how it affects the meaning of the base word.

A morphemic approach to be successful should be dealt in exactly the same way as a phonic one, that is using multi-sensory learning and following a structured cumulative programme. It is best to begin with 's' followed by 'ing' and 'ed' and the rule 'Just Add'. This becomes possible once you have done final blends. Flash cards are essential to reinforce the spelling pattern and a definition card for a suffix and base/root word so that you are able to communicate effectively. It is also essential that you use the right 'jargon' – the terms noun, verb etc. when discussing how the suffix changes the base.

| - s | - ing | - ed | Use an appropriate word as a 'cue' in the form of a picture on the reverse side such as 'plants', 'planting' and 'planted'. |
|-----|-------|------|----|

NB At this stage the 'ed' will be pronounced as a syllable.

These suffixes are from 'Old English', as are the majority of the everyday ones and as such are best taught first using a synthetic method such as having the learner build longer words from individual morphemes. For example, how many words can he make using these suffixes and words ending in 'ck'?

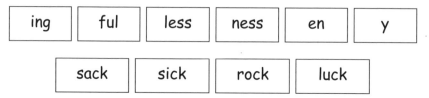

This shows how simple it is to tie morphemes into a particular spelling pattern. Encourage the addition of two suffixes where it is possible – stickers, thickening. When you feel your learner is ready introduce prefixes but again keep to the Old English ones of 'un' (not or opposite) and 'mis' – unbending, misspelling.

Once he is confident with the synthetic approach, work on the analytical method. In this instance teach him to highlight the suffix and underline the base word.

<u>rust</u>**ed**     <u>sad</u>**ness**     <u>trick</u>**y**     <u>fast</u>**en**     <u>send</u>**ing**

In spelling, first ask the learner to say the whole word and then split into base word and suffix. As he writes them, a pause between the two parts will help reinforce the base word and suffix.

Older learners, especially those who are at secondary school will benefit from the next level, that of Latin morphemes. In this case the structure of the word will be prefix-root-suffix. The meaning of the root is not always apparent. For example, 'inject' is made up of the prefix 'in' and root 'ject' and literally translated means 'to throw in'. If it were 'injection' then the 'ion' suffix simply denotes a noun.

In many cases it is possible to work out the meaning of the root using everyday words. In tractor, the root 'tract' means to draw or pull which is what the dentist will do when he extracts a tooth!

Again, flash cards are invaluable except that you will need to include the root word as well as the affixes.

| tract | To pull, draw  | ex | out EXIT |
|---|---|---|---|

Use the same synthetic and analytic approaches to word structure and it will soon be apparent how many words can be made from just a few parts and include the Old English suffixes. Latin endings 'ion', 'ive', 'ise' can be covered later.

| See how many words you can make | | |
|---|---|---|
| **prefix** | **root** | **suffix** |
| sub con re ex in | tract ject tend sist | s ed ing |

The Greek level will suit any age in terms of reading and vocabulary development but is often tricky for spelling. However, it is essential for learners studying on GCSE and A level science courses. Greek words usually take the form of compound words such as 'astro – naut' – 'sailor of the stars'. The best approach with this vocabulary is to begin with a word such as 'telephone' and work on how many other words can be made using the 'tele' (distance) morpheme. You could even try the word 'cacography'!

Finding out how words work using their origins and meaning is fascinating and rewarding for both teacher and learner. It is not a case of teaching him a different way of tackling reading and spelling, rather the same one that enables others to master written English effectively. This is the means by which my learner graduated to 'oesophagus'. Simultaneously you will be showing just how transparent English is if you learn the rules differently.

The focus in the Rose Report on the 'phonic'-based approach to reading and spelling is a very good start. But it is not the whole picture. We must be careful that this emphasis does not mean we will be 'throwing the baby out with the bath water!'

You don't have to be a rocket scientist to use this approach – a good dictionary, a sense of adventure and this very quick introduction is all that is required. For those of you who would like a little more information before tackling this, the following books are invaluable:

Marcia, K. & Henry, P. (2003) *Unlocking Literacy: Effective Decoding & Spelling Instruction.* ISBN 1-55766-64-4

Ramsden, M. (1993) *Rescuing Spelling.* ISBN 1-85741-090-4

# Tips for Supporting Dyscalculic Children

Gillian Cawse

Dyscalculia is thought to affect between 3% and 6% of the population and it is important to be able to identify it and put in place a remedial programme. One of the problems of identification is distinguishing what might be dyscalculia and what might be other reasons for difficulties, such as those associated with dyslexia or dyspraxia. It seems that the essential elements are the lack of 'feel' for numbers, the number system and lack of progress with conventional remedial instruction. A simple checklist is:

- Having difficulty with the direct retrieval of number facts.

- Making counting errors.

- Relying on immature strategies such as finger counting and making errors with these.

- Slow speed of processing of numerical information.

- An inability to estimate.

- A poor knowledge of the worth or value of a number.

- A poor grasp of procedures and concepts.

- A poor sequential memory for numbers and operations.

- An inability to see patterns in numbers, e.g. if 10, 20, 30, 40 then it follows 12, 22, 32, 42.

- A poor grasp of the 10s base of the number system.

- Trouble moving up and down the numberline or number square.

## Intervention Strategies

There are three things to consider with any intervention strategy: programme content, lesson structure and method of delivery.

The key features of an intervention programme are similar to those employed for the development of literacy skills for a person with dyslexia; that is, it should be multi-sensory, structured and cumulative.

## Programme Content

A critical first stage for the pupil with dyscalculia must be the inclusion of work on numbers and the number system. These pupils lack an intuitive grasp of these and have no natural 'feel' for quantities. A good programme will include work on the concepts of 'bigger than' and 'smaller than' and the tens structure of the number system. Pupils should be able to start seeing patterns in the number system and to generalise sequences so that, for example, from 10, 20, 30, 40, 50, you can derive 12, 22, 32, 42, 52. Pupils should be able to count in tens, twos and fives, both forwards and backwards.

Learning to get a 'feel' for numbers and the number system is critical for the pupil with dyscalculia and this section of the programme is probably the key element that differentiates one devised for learners with dyscalculia from more general mathematics support programmes.

The programme should be structured and cumulative, proceeding in small steps with lots of repetition and regular review. It should concentrate to some extent on the number skills that are needed for life such as time, money and weight. These are long-term aims. Initial aims should focus on learning some key facts such as number bonds to ten, double numbers to 40, near doubles, adding 9 and adding 8. The pupil can then use these facts to derive others. Similarly with times table facts, it is unlikely that they will ever have direct recall of these, so certain key elements should be learnt such as 2, 5 and 10, square numbers and 9 times using the finger method and the 4 times table by doubling doubles.

## Lesson Structure

The lessons should have a clearly defined structure to them so that students know and understand what is going to happen. A typical lesson will have the following format:

- **Sequencing or number system activity**. This is a good starter as it is vital for pupils with dyscalculia that their knowledge of the number system and patterns within it can be secure. It could include such activities as counting in twos, fives and tens both forwards and backwards, sorting numbers from smallest to largest, numberline and number square activities. These activities can be built into games.

- **Maths packs routine**. This will take the form of a pack of cards that can be built up over time as new facts and topics are covered. It should include some key number facts, symbols and terminology. The question will be on one side and the answer on the reverse. For example, on the front 'double 8' is written and on the reverse '16'. With some material, such as converting fractions to decimals or percentages, the cards can be tested both ways. It is important that they make the cards themselves; this is part of the learning process. The pack could be taken away to practise at home. It can be a useful activity for all age groups.

- **Revision of previous learning**. This should be a point from the previous lesson or previous learning linked to the new teaching point. It could take the form of a game or worksheet.

- **New teaching point**. The topic should be introduced using concrete materials and move on to recording and symbolic representation. A 'scaffolding' approach should be used, giving lots of help to start with and then reducing input as the pupil becomes more confident. When the point is grasped (it may take more than one lesson), ask if they can then teach it back to you. Small steps are important.

- **Reinforcement activity**. This may take the form of a game or worksheet.

You should be prepared to repeat each point perhaps every half term or term, setting aside time for this.

A final note; maths is an incremental subject and there may be unexpected gaps in a pupil's knowledge, so any lesson plan has to be flexible, you may have to abandon everything to recap and concentrate on a lower-level skill.

## Methods of Delivery

This is perhaps the most critical feature of a programme. The teaching should be multi-sensory so that the pupil sees, says, does and writes every aspect of the lesson. The pupil should be encouraged to talk through what they are doing and, where possible, employ directed-discovery style learning. At the end of a topic the pupils should be in a position where they can communicate their learning to someone else.

There are a wide variety of concrete materials that can be used, from simple counters and coins (glass nuggets are good as they are quite tactile), to bead strings, peg boards and the abacus. The Slavonic Abacus is particularly good as it divides, by the use of colour, each row into fives. Base ten materials are particularly useful for working with the tens structure of the number system. 'Numicon' is a commercial product that can be used to carry out a wide range of arithmetical activities and to aid understanding of the number system. It comes with its own teaching programme. Cuisenaire Rods can have a multitude of uses such as in the teaching of number bonds, factors, multiples, fractions, area and perimeter.

Rhymes and visual images can be used to help learn key number facts, for example, 'gate and shoe = 8 + 2' as part of a sequence for learning number bonds to ten. The pupil can draw the images on cards and include them in their maths pack. Similarly, something like 'four floors licked clean (4 x 4 = 16)' can be tried for square numbers. Visual images and rhyme are powerful memory tools.

Learning can be reinforced by the use of games and software such as 'Numbershark'. The Woodlands Junior School website has many free games on it. Worksheets help to practise and consolidate learning but care should be taken in their layout. It is essential not to fit too much on a page and there should be room to write down any calculations. It is useful to include some worksheet practice as this is a link with classroom mathematics, but the material included should always be achievable for the pupil; pupils with dyscalculia will often have a history of failure with such work and it is vital to increase their self-esteem.

## Resources

Numicon: **http://www.numicon.com**

Woodlands Junior School Website: **http://www.woodlands-junior.kent.sch.uk/maths**

Slavonic Abacus: **http://xavier.bangor.ac.uk/xavier/swgal/abacus/index.html** (site includes free interactive version with some worksheets).

Cuisenaire Rods: Available from Amazon and e-bay

Numbershark: **http://www.wordshark.co.uk/numbershark.html** . Also available through Amazon.

# Memory Strategies

Caroline Bark

*'It takes me much longer than everyone else to revise and I find it really hard to learn new things.'*

When I ask students who come to me for assessment what it is they would most like help with, this is one of the most frequent responses. Here are some strategies they feel really work for them. These strategies are concerned with encoding, consolidation and retrieval from long-term memory.

- Pupils should be encouraged to develop their meta-cognitive skills in relation to memory strategies. What works for one learner will not necessarily work for another. Our role is to introduce them to a range of methods, provide examples of when and how they might use the strategy and ensure they are able to use them correctly. Develop a personal memory dictionary with your learner. This could include a list of strategies. One may be recording facts that need to be learnt in their own voice, possibly on a mobile phone and playing it back to themselves. Discuss and record the type of information that may best be learnt in this way, for example, times tables. Provide an area for evaluation so that they record their thoughts on whether this particular strategy was effective or how it may be adapted. Alternatively, learners could develop a mind map of strategies that have been found to be useful to them in different situations. This could then be used for reference when revising for exams.

- Try and ensure that information is transformed from one sensory mode to another. Transforming information means that it has to be closely analysed; the salient points have to be extracted and the relationship of different parts of the information to each other has to be assessed. Different senses are used and, therefore, different areas of the brain. Information is more likely to be consolidated and retained.

- One method of transforming information is for learners to imagine they have to deliver a short lesson explaining a topic, e.g. the digestive system. To complete this task visual information, including diagrams and text, has to be transferred to verbal information. In order to verbalise an idea you have to truly understand it. It is important to speak aloud; otherwise you can skim over areas you don't thoroughly understand. This process highlights areas of misunderstanding. This is important, as learners are not always aware that they don't understand something until they are forced to analyse their thinking in this way. Speaking aloud has an additional benefit for learners with language difficulties. It allows them to become familiar with the words and phrases, which will enable them to express their ideas more fluently in an exam or time-bound situation. By actually articulating the words they are more likely to remember them.

- Another example of transforming information would be using a mind map to help learn information from a textbook. The process of identifying the main ideas in the text for the branches of the mind map, possibly through the use of topic sentences, forces learners to create a structure for the information. Then reducing the ideas into salient visual images and keywords ensures that the meaning of the text is thoroughly processed. Once the mind map is complete the information could be transformed once again into a verbal format by talking through each branch aloud.

- It is important that the process of revision results in some kind of product, that the learner has a tangible result at the end of a set period of time. This might be in the form of a diagram, a set of revision cards, a tape, a mind map, a set of question cards or a photocopied and highlighted section of a textbook. A product means revision has a short-term goal, it keeps the learner motivated, it is satisfying and the product can be used to revisit the information at a later date.

- Memories are consolidated by repetition, by revisiting the information. This is not good news to most students as it sounds like more work. Show them the Forgetting Curve.

Provide some shocking statistics 'If it is not reviewed then only about 20% of new information will be remembered the next day'. Emphasise that information can be reduced when it is revisited. Bullet points, keywords, flow charts, mind maps are all helpful. Help them set up a formal timetable. Explain this will save them time in the long run!

- Always encourage learners to study in short time slots with planned breaks in between. This is good news! We remember most from the beginnings and endings of learning sessions (primacy and recency effect). So plenty of beginnings and endings mean more opportunities for increased learning.

- New information is much easier to remember if it can be linked to existing knowledge. It helps provide a scaffold for their memory and allow them to make associations. Encourage students to think about what they already know about this topic or related topics. For example, in history they could try and relate the period of an event to other events by the use of a timeline. Rote material can be especially hard to remember. Explain that facts and figures can be made much easier to learn if they are associated with something meaningful. The classic 'I ate and ate till I was sick on the floor (8 x 8 =64)' works because it is amusing, easy to visualise and it sounds similar to the facts to be learnt. If dates and names have to be learnt, try and link these to information which is relevant to the student.

- Some students have difficulty consolidating and retrieving information because they find it hard to categorise it when it is encoded. They may need help creating a mental filing system so that information can be more easily located and retrieved when needed. Draw up a chart with an overview of the topic to be learnt. Ensure that revision aids such as glossaries, revision cards and mind maps are physically stored in related areas. Don't flit from one area of revision to another, try and memorise related information in the same or adjacent study periods. Use colour, font type, visual icons and different stationery to try and group related information.

# The Centre Academy Schools

## "The most unique and most successful special needs schools in the UK"

The Centre Academy Schools, CA London and CA East Anglia, enable students with specific learning difficulties to reclaim their futures. We do so by teaching the skills and coping strategies that students with Dyslexia and other learning challenges require in order to succeed.

With small classes (usually 5 or 6 students), significant one-to-one instruction, and dedicated, highly experienced teachers, the Centre Academy Schools make it possible for all students to work to their fullest potential by designing a programme of instruction tailored to meet the individual student's needs.

Literacy and numeracy form the core of a pupil's studies. We are dedicated to ensuring that our students become careful, active readers. Our commitment to Maths is equally strong, and our students benefit from a programme that blends regular class-based study with individualised instruction. Other areas of study are the Humanities, Science, ICT, Art, Drama, Music, PSHE, Citizenship, Foreign Languages, RE, Media Studies and Study Skills.

Our curriculum is especially unique, as we offer *both* the British National Curriculum through GCSE and the American High School Diploma; the Diploma is not examination-based, but instead uses a continuous assessment system, thereby minimising the anxiety that special needs students frequently suffer when faced with the pressures of examinations. Our GCSE students have a 100 percent record of acceptance to sixth form and other colleges. Diploma graduates regularly receive unconditional offers to universities throughout the UK.

**CA London:** co-educational day school, ages 9-18; total enrolment 60; admits students with a variety of learning challenges on a case-by-case basis; urban environment enabling students to profit from the capital's cultural, artistic and historic possibilities.

**CA East Anglia:** co-educational day and boarding school, ages 8-16; total enrolment 40; admits students with a variety of learning challenges on a case-by-case basis. Elegant classroom buildings and excellent boarding facilities; acres of playing fields provide the ideal setting for extensive sports and activities programmes.

Centre Academy London
92 St John's Hill,
Battersea, London SW11 1SH

Tel: 020 7738 2344 Fax: 020 7738 9862
Email: info@centreacademy.net
www.centreacademy.net

Centre Academy East Anglia
Church Road
Brettenham, Suffolk IP7 7QR

Tel: 01449 736404 Fax: 01449 737881
Email: admin@centreacademy.net
www.centreacademy.net

- Conversely, try and keep similar but unrelated information as separate as possible. Memories can be disrupted or obscured by subsequent learning, particularly where the new information is similar to the old information. 'Si' in Spanish and 'oui' in French are very likely to be confused. Use different colours, stationery, study times and even study location if possible!

- Help your students create retrieval cues to access material from long-term memory. This may be a visual image, a movement, or a verbal mnemonic. Ideally, work with them to help construct relevant associations that will help them access the new information through more than one sensory channel.

*'The existence of forgetting has never been proved; We only know that some things don't come to mind when we want them.' (Friedrich Nietzsche)*

Spend time with your students educating them about effective methods of encoding and consolidation and evaluating what works best for them. They will be rewarded by an improved ability to get *'things to come to mind when they want them'!*

# Secondary School Support for Dyslexic Learners: Impetus and Initiatives

Geraldine Price

There has never been a more exciting time for dyslexic secondary school students. A growing awareness of their needs has been well acknowledged in the legislation, official documents, professional association guidance and recent Department for Children, Schools and Families (DCSF) reports. The message is clear to teachers; dyslexia-friendly learning environments are essential (BDA 1999 Dyslexia-Friendly School Packs; SEN in the Disability Discrimination Act (SENDA) 2001; Department for Education & Skills (DfES) 2002 SEN Code of Practice; and the recently published Rose Report 2009).

> 'Schools are expected to respond to the diverse needs of all students, to provide a 'dyslexia-friendly learning environment' together with a guarantee of support and services to match these needs. There should be staff designated with responsibility for co-ordinating special needs provision in each school'. DfES SEN Code of Practice (2002).

Sir Jim Rose's review (2009) has provided detailed information relating to the needs of secondary school dyslexic learners in Chapter 5: Tackling difficulties beyond reading that are also associated with dyslexia.

However, increasing the awareness of the subject teacher of the needs of the dyslexic learner is one half of the support equation. Schools need to consider an holistic approach to support, to provide positive learning environments to enable our dyslexic students to maximise their potential.

# The
# **MOAT**SCHOOL

## An Aspirational Secondary Day-School
## for Children with Specific Learning Difficulties

Founded in 1998 The Moat School is London's first co-educational secondary school for dyslexic children offering an intensive and structured learning programme teaching the national curriculum.

Children receive a totally inclusive education, they understand their difficulties, but thrive academically, emotionally and socially in spite of them. Pupils have individual timetables that address their needs, and creative talent is nurtured in small classes enabling success in public examinations. The Moat School is CReSTED registered and has been described as the 'Gold Standard' in SpLD education.

The Good Schools Guide says: "Something special. Not for children wanting to be cosseted and comforted, but a hard-working haven for bright, determined dyslexics and dyspraxics who know what they want from life and will achieve when given a chance".

## Come and see for yourself

Bishop's Avenue, Fulham, London SW6 6EG
**T**: 020 7610 9018　**F**: 020 7610 9098
office@moatschool.org.uk　**www.moatschool.org.uk**

## Linking Support to the Curriculum Context

By the time they reach secondary school, many dyslexic learners have begun the slow route to decoding and encoding. Most still need help with basic literacy skills to increase fluency and accuracy, so will need to follow a phonological and morphological fast-track language programme. Nevertheless, as the curriculum demands grow, they will need an additional type of support. Keeping up with many different subject teachers in class and the greater complexities of homework puts pressure upon weak working memory skills which have an impact upon personal organisation and process organisation. Appropriate support for independent management of learning is an essential key to achieving good results and developing greater self-esteem. Thus, support needs to be focused on developing skills to ensure that these students can keep up with their peers in class and obtain results which they think they deserve. Therefore, a *continuum of support* is required, linked to current curriculum demands so that techniques can be gradually introduced to provide vital skills for access.

At secondary level, all pupils need to be able to:

■ Comprehend texts.

■ Communicate effectively for different subject audiences.

■ Take notes efficiently.

■ Make notes as part of written communication and project work.

■ Organise work for deadlines.

■ Revise for examinations.

The underlying skills for these activities are:

■ Functional literacy – higher order skills.

■ Organisation of processes.

■ Memory.

- Estimation of time taken for tasks.

A support package for these students should, therefore, encompass teaching techniques to develop, strengthen and compensate through curriculum access. If the focus is upon the demands of the curriculum, the dyslexic students immediately see the relevance of the skills they are learning because they can put them into practice in class and with homework tasks. This also shifts the attention from the individual to the wider context; it is no longer about what the dyslexic student cannot do, but rather about what he needs to develop to access the curriculum.

Higher order reading skills provide the basis for functionality. Alongside the teaching of decoding skills for fluency and efficiency, the dyslexic learner must be aware of the underlying skills which ensure deeper levels of comprehension and criticality. These skills need to be explicitly modelled by the support tutor but also talked about and reinforced by subject teachers so that the dyslexic student can immediately see their application.

## Reading Skills

For secondary school students, a two-pronged approach is necessary: increasing decoding skills and developing higher order skills. Most dyslexic secondary school pupils require a balance of these two aspects, matched to individual need. Ultimately there is a need to teach the underlying skills so that dyslexic readers, despite weak fluency and processing speeds, can learn to become critical readers. Thus, these students need to be EXPLICITLY taught how to monitor comprehension of a text and how to access text information more efficiently.

## Higher Order Skills for Reading Tasks:

- Retrieving information.

- Searching/selection of information.

- Skimming.

- Scanning.

- Categorisation of information.

- Organising/mapping information.

- Inference skills.

- Summary skills.

- Planning.

- Knowledge of texts.

- Importance of an overview.

- Knowledge of text layouts (deconstruction of texts to learn how experts put texts together).

- Knowledge of linguistic features.

- Knowledge of the role of keywords.

- Knowledge of different reading styles and how to use them flexibly.

- Confidence to tackle the activity your way.

Curriculum support needs to be carefully orchestrated with subject teachers so the above skills are introduced at relevant stages. The use of current subject content materials provides the foundation for skill acquisition.

- Task analysis approach as opposed to the scattergun approach – purpose of task.

- Overview techniques.

- Prediction techniques.

- Knowledge of paragraph structure.

- Knowledge of how language is used in different contexts.

# Writing Skills

Similarly, the development of writing/compositional skills needs to be modelled so that the hidden, cognitive processes are made explicit. Scaffolding support for writing in the real academic context provides the dyslexic writer with the over-learning and reinforcement so vital to progression. Dyslexic writers need to be exposed to the decision making involved in the production of text so that they have a repertoire of techniques which they can draw upon to get on with writing. For example, making notes is a skill which involves linguistic processes which put the dyslexic writer under pressure because of weak working memory and poor word retrieval skills. Often, the dyslexic student uses one note-making system which has worked once and then finds that, as the curriculum demands increase, they slavishly use this one system which may not be the right one for the job in hand. Thus, they need to be exposed to a number of techniques for note-making (Price & Maier (2007) *pp 80 – 100 (*the pros and cons of different methods and gives advice about when they can be used most effectively). They need to develop their own writing frames – the rationale for making these frames is vital to supporting weak memory. By participating in the thinking process, the writing frame becomes a real memory and organisation tool rather than a mechanistic frame for writing. Many teachers simply dish out a writing frame and some poor writers only use these and never progress to the next stage of writing. In this way a dependency culture is encouraged.

## Dyslexia-friendly Classroom Environments

Positive teaching and learning environments can be achieved and need to be taken in the context of manageable solutions. Busy subject teachers need to be aware that what works for some dyslexic learners will work for other specific learning difficulties because of the co-occurrence of needs. Adjustments to the classroom environment can make a substantial difference (Rose 2009, Chapter 5). The quality of the learning experience can be greatly improved by:

■ Considering how and when instructions are given in a lesson.

- Complementing verbal instructions with numbered bullet points.

- Providing alternative formats.

- Posters which provide constant reminders of the correct spelling of key subject vocabulary and mathematical signs and formulae.

- Worksheets produced on pale blue and place yellow coloured paper (Stein 2003).

- Adjusted activities for homework. This may be accepting an alternative format for responses to demonstrate knowledge and understanding.

Many subject teachers welcome guidelines to help them in the production of worksheets:

- Use of comic sans font is easier on the eye for those with reading difficulties.

- Key vocabulary in **bold** text.

- Use of colour – keywords, for example, could always be in red. This ensures that these words stand out and those with hesitant reading skills can be taught to skim more effectively.

- Layout of written text – uncluttered information is easier to access for those with literacy difficulties. If you put boxes around information you will help the students to 'see' that certain information is linked and goes together.

- Visual representations in tandem with prose.

- Talking worksheets – these are ways of providing a multi-sensory environment. Your worksheets can be accessed by the 'read back' facilities of a number of computer programs.

## In Conclusion

The shift from concentrating upon decoding and encoding skills (lower order) to providing skill support which can be directly applied to the curriculum has given much needed encouragement to dyslexic learners in secondary schools. Tapping into the strengths of reasoning and creativity, by adopting a decision-making, problem-solving approach to becoming an independent learner appeals to dyslexic students who need to boost both academic performance and self-esteem.

## References

BDA (1999) *The BDA Quality Mark Initiative for LEAs: The Dyslexia-Friendly Standards*

DCSF (2008) *Personalised Learning – A Practical Guide.*

DCSF (2009) *Identifying And Teaching Children And Young People With Dyslexia And Literacy Difficulties.* An independent report from Sir Jim Rose to the Secretary of State for Children, Schools and Families.

DfES (2002) *Special Educational Needs Code of Practice*

Price, G.A. & Maier, P. (2007) *Effective Study Skills: Unlock Your Potential.* London, Pearson Education.

SENDA: *Special Educational Needs and the Disability Act* (2001)

Stein, J. (2003) Visual Motion Sensitivity and Reading. *Neuropsychologia*, 41: 1785–1793

# ADHD Teaching and Management

Fin O'Regan

Attention Deficit Hyperactivity Disorder (ADHD) is an internationally validated medical condition of brain dysfunction in which individuals have difficulties in controlling impulses, inhibiting appropriate behaviour and sustaining attention. The net result of this is educational, behavioural, social and related difficulties.

Though controversy about the term persists, particularly through the media, the National Institute of Clinical Excellence NICE in 2008 clearly stated that, 'ADHD is a heterogeneous behavioural syndrome' and that, 'teachers who have received training about ADHD and its management should provide behavioural interventions in the classroom to help children and young persons with ADHD'. For the full report see **www.nice.org.uk**

The full diagnostic criteria regarding ADHD are listed in The Fourth Edition of the American Psychiatric Association (DSM IV) in 1994 but the 'triad' of core features are as follows:

1) Poor Attention Span.

2) Excessive Impulsivity.

3) Hyperactivity.

Symptoms of attention may include being disorganised, being forgetful, easily distracted and finding it difficult to sustain attention in tasks or play activities while hyperactive or impulsive behaviours may include fidgeting, having trouble playing quietly, interrupting others and always being on the go. While such behaviours exist in all of us from time to time the difference is the degree and intensity in specific individuals.

Though opinions differ, research indicates that about 5% of the school-aged population is affected to some degree by ADHD of which approximately 1% are severely hyperactive. In addition

30–40% of all children referred for professional help because of behaviour problems come with presenting complaints associated with ADHD. The considered ratio of boys to girls is somewhere in the region of 4:1.

Specific learning difficulties such as dyslexia, dyspraxia and dyscalculia occur in approximately 40% of children with ADHD while disruptive behavioural disorders such as Oppositional Defiant Disorder and Conduct Disorder occur in about 50% of cases. Finally, anxiety disorders occur in about 30% of all ADHD individuals.

## Education and Social Interaction

Many factors are needed to help children with ADHD cope with educational, behavioural and social aspects of school. It is important to mention that a full range of issues must be considered; for example, there is no point in planning some one-to-one pre-school support if it is unlikely that child will get to school in time because his mother cannot get him out of bed and onto the bus.

Though academic and behavioural issues within the school programme appear high on the agenda, a main area of concern of children with ADHD will be interaction with other children.

Initially, pupils with ADHD can appear quite amusing within a group of learners but this 'class clown' effect soon wears thin to be replaced by impatience and intolerance of the constant interruptions that can take place. This can lead to isolation of the individual from the peer group.

In addition, many problems for children with ADHD stem from their inability to handle various degrees of environmental stimuli that come their way. This is why they operate best in a consistent structure providing them with safety and security to stay on task and out of trouble.

Therefore, consideration must be given to all non-classroom time such as break/lunch-time and sports/activities where socialisation problems between learners can and will occur. It is recommended that break times be as structured as much as possible, scheduling effective staff to supervise.

Though the term ADHD is not included within the SEN Code of Practice, the Disability and Discrimination Act (2003) which complements the Revised Code of 2001 provides clear guidance that ADHD is a disability and thus must be managed within schools, the workplace and the community.

For day-to-day management of learners with ADHD in the classroom, specific tried-and-trusted strategies and suggestions are listed below. In some cases this will simply confirm good practice but the key is to develop consistent routines and rituals for learning but remain flexible with some of the minor distractions and incidents that will occur.

Key strategies that should be employed include (the learner is referred to as *he* or *him* for ease of style):

- Seat him near teacher but include as part of the regular class.

- Place him up front with his back to the rest of the class keeping others out of view.

- Allow him to use manipulatives when sitting to help concentration.

- Surround him with good role models, preferably those seen as 'Significant Others'. Encourage peer tutoring and co-operative learning.

- Avoid distracting stimuli. Try not to place him near heaters, doors or windows, high traffic areas, gas taps etc. in science lab etc.

- These children do not handle change well so avoid transitions, changes in schedule, physical relocation, (monitor closely on field trips).

- Be creative! Produce a stimuli-reduced area or 'work station' for learners to access.

- Maintain eye contact with him during verbal instruction.

- Make directions clear and concise. Be consistent with daily instructions.

- Make sure he comprehends before beginning the task.

- Help him to feel comfortable with seeking assistance.

- These children need support for a longer period of time than normal. Gradually reduce assistance.

- Require a daily assignment notebook. Ensure he writes the assignment and parents/ teachers sign daily for homework tasks.

- Give one task at a time but monitor frequently.

- Modify assignments as necessary. Develop an individualised programme for specific subjects.

- Consider the proactive use of headsets for individualised work as a proactive distraction.

- Break assignments down into chunks.

- Encourage controlled movement during class time.

- Make use of computerised programmes and resources for learning objectives.

- Make sure you test knowledge, not attention span.

For more information see ADHD *plus* page at **www.fintanoregan.com**

## Medication and Working with Parents

Medication is one option that may be considered for management for children with ADHD. As stated in the NICE guidelines: 'Drug treatment for children with ADHD should always form part of a comprehensive treatment plan that includes psychological, behavioural and educational advice and interventions'.

Essentially there are two main kinds of treatment options for ADHD which we can classify as the:

- Stimulants – Methylphenidate and Dexamfetamine.

- Non Stimulants – Atomoxetine.

All schools should have their own 'medicines policy' for the storage and administration of medicines.

For any child on medication, communication between family, physician and school is crucial. Although the decision as to whether medication is prescribed is with the physician, the role of the family working with school is essential to monitor successful outcomes for the child.

As a result, positive communication channels with parents are vital and frequent telephone/text contact, parent-teacher conferences and possibly daily report cards are all vehicles to be considered.

Parents may ask what they should do at home. One of the best ways to handle this is to direct them toward the large number of home management materials available from 'ADDISS', the national ADHD advocacy for children and families with ADHD (see **www.addiss.co.uk**). They provide home management products for children with ADHD.

Educating these children can be difficult and demanding but also extremely fulfilling. The key is to develop a compromise between adapting the school environment to the needs of the child as well as helping him to adapt to demands of the school environment.

# Dyslexia and Contemporary (Modern Popular) Music

Glynis Lavington

## Introduction

Although there is growing interest as to how dyslexia affects musicians, knowledge and research within this field is still in its infancy. For the dyslexic student key strengths often centre on a natural and innate talent for musical creativity and imaginative and innovative thinking. However, the very fact that dyslexia is an individual combination of abilities and difficulties leads to varying disparities in performance. This situation inevitably leads to confusion, not only for the student but also for music educators. We have all come across the situation, the learner who is struggling despite clear ability in some areas of the curriculum. The aim of this article is to highlight some of the areas of potential difficulty, providing a brief overview.

In order to understand the potential challenges facing the dyslexic musician, it is important to consider the context of their studies and the processes the student needs to carry out in order to perform and progress.

## Context

There are various differences in performance requirements with regard to contemporary (modern popular) music. For example, music is often traditionally handed down from generation to generation with many pieces being learnt by ear. As a result the student may well have learnt to play by ear and is less likely to have studied the written language in the form of music notation. However, within the context of contemporary music at higher education level, the student is required to read notation.

## Challenges

One of the challenges for the dyslexic student is learning to read and decode the written language of music; lack of mastery experience within this context leads to confusion over which strategies to adopt. This confusion is compounded for the dyslexic student who is highly compensated within their first language, especially if the compensations have been developed unknowingly without a metacognitive approach. As a result secondary characteristics can develop, causing anxiety and stress, which inevitably have an impact on the confidence levels of the student when asked to perform. The students are often very aware of their difficulties as the comments below indicate; however, their understanding as to why this should be the case is most often lacking. It is, therefore, vitally important to identify factors that provide explanations for the dyslexic student, as to why they find certain tasks more difficult than their non-dyslexic peers.

## Comments from Dyslexic Students

'It feels like sight-reading every time I look at it.'

'I look at a note and then I play the wrong one.'

'The lines blur and move.'

'I lose my place.'

'I lost count.'

'I read the key signature and now there is an accidental, what was the key signature again?'

The student is required to memorise and recall information at speed and adjust from the familiar to the unknown within their new environment. It is the requirement for automaticity and fluency that often presents the greatest challenge, particularly when the student is asked to perform on the spur of the moment and especially when under a time constraint. The musician is required to simultaneously decode visual information into motor activity, which can be broken down as follows:

- Recognise and process the vast quantity of information on the page, which includes symbols and instructions relating

# OLYMPUS

# High quality audio processing

The DM-5 delivers everything that you expect from an Olympus audio recorder... and then some. With its incredible 8GB of internal memory the DM-5 supports over 2,000 hours of recording and allows plenty of storage for your favourite music. It also supports DAISY (Digital Accessible Information System) and speciality software that converts textbooks into speech for the blind and dyslexic. With the new Visual Index feature and 2.2" full collour LCD screen, the DM-5 takes recording to a whole new level.

## DM-5 Key Features

■ MULTIPLE RECORDING FORMATS
Enables high quality recording, no additional software required. Records in MP3, PCM and WMA formats; plays back in MP3, PCM, WMA and Audible file formats.

■ 2.2 INCH FULL COLOUR LCD
The bright 2.2" colour screen enables clear, easy navigation of menus and files. And when using the DM-5 as a music player you have the ability to see the album cover and artist name.

■ BATTERY CHARGE FUNCTION
Charges the battery while connected to your PC or plugged in the AC Adapter (included). Long 20-hour battery life with lithium-ion rechargeable battery.

■ VISUAL INDEX FUNCTION
Download images to be used as your wallpaper, view colour images, or link images to your recorded audio files to create a visual index.

■ 8GB INTERNAL MEMORY
8GB of internal memory allows you 2,000 worry-free hours of recording time, with microSD card compatibility that extends it up to16GB.

■ MP3, WMA & PCM RECORDING
Record and play back in MP3, WMA and PCM formats with a quality that's as good as its operation is easy.

■ VOICE RECOGNITION
Use simple voice commands to create calendar entries, to-do lists and other basic functions.

■ VOICE GUIDANCE
A voice guidance system ensures seamless, user-friendly operation of all functions in the menu.

■ MULTIPLE FORMATS
Supports Daisy, audible.com, podcasting and audio book formats.

■ MULTIPLE LANGUAGE DISPLAY
The bright LCD supports and displays three languages -- another plus for accessibility.

■ 20 HOURS OF BATTERY LIFE
There's up to 20 hours of recording capability with the DM-5's long-life battery. The battery can be charged when you hook the recorder up to your computer via the USB port or when you plug in the AC Adapter (included).

■ USB CONNECTION COMPATIBLE WITH PC AND MAC
Uploads files directly to your PC or MAC using a simple cable connection, while the USB 2.0 High-Speed Storage feature allows fast transfers and mass storage of files.

■ OLYMPUS SONORITY
Edit your files with Olympus Sonority sound editing software (included), which is compatible with PCs and MACs.

to rhythm, pitch, tone, speed and general feel of the piece (directions can often be in one of at least four languages).

■ Recognise and process the auditory input as rhythm and melody.

■ Act on it (perform) by translation of the notation into precisely timed movements.

## Individual Differences

Underlying individual differences can have a significant impact on the student's abilities, although this is not always assumed to be the case with regard to music. It is, therefore, vitally important that these differences; both strengths and weaknesses, are identified and explained to the student. Areas that should be explored are those relating to the processing of information, both auditory and visual, speed of processing, ability to multitask, co-ordination, spatial ability, sequencing, working memory and automaticity and fluency in output. Information gained from the student's diagnostic report can be useful in highlighting possible areas of difficulty and can help provide explanations for the student for example:

## Weaknesses in Visual/Non-verbal Profile:

■ Following a sequence of instructions in diagrammatic form (notation).

■ Breaking the piece into component parts.

■ Discriminating, recalling and learning associations between abstract symbols.

■ Keeping their place in the score.

■ Distortions.

■ Processing speed and fluency.

■ Eye-hand co-ordination.

■ Copying from the board.

Difficulties do not always centre on visual processing difficulties, slower auditory processing speeds can also have an impact. Research suggests that auditory analysis requires both hemispheres of the brain to work simultaneously in order to identify rhythm, pitch and tone. This can have an impact on the student's ability to play the piece, name the notes and chords, or write in notated form.

In order to notate accurately the student needs to remember the symbol to write and the position on the stave. Co-ordination and spatial difficulties can exacerbate this situation. For example, pitch is annotated by the position of the symbols on the page, which requires spatial reasoning, e.g. up = higher sounds, whereas fingers may need to move across and down or along and down (guitar) to create a higher sound. Reading time signatures (looks like a fraction) can also present problems. Which number goes at the top? Which is at the bottom?

## Sequencing Problems

- Names of the notes follow the alphabetic sequence A–G and then repeat through the octave, H does not come after G.

- Instructions such as 'start at the 3rd line of the 2nd bar'.

- Remembering the sequence of movement.

- Repeat signs indicate notes, chords, bar or bars to be repeated.

## Memory

- Memorising and recalling long passages of music or several new pieces in a short time frame.

- Learning musical structures and rules (syntax of the language).

## Tuition and Support

It is vital that the student develops a metacognitive approach to their studies. By gaining an understanding of their individual differences and through the development of metacognitive skills, the student is able to build their own toolbox of strategies, which ultimately will enable them to take an independent approach to their studies. After all, whilst reasonable adjustments are possible, the student will need to be able to cope during live performances and in a studio situation.

## Practical Approaches:

- Analysis of the task. What is the student being asked to do? (Input, cognition, output).

- Multi-sensory methods.

- Coloured overlays/coloured paper (visual perceptual difficulties).

- Enabling technology, ear training & notation software, digital recorders.

- Reasonable adjustments, delivery and assessment methods.

- Develop a reciprocal working relationship with the music tutor.

## Conclusion

Whilst knowledge and research is still in its infancy within this context there is increasing evidence suggesting that both language and music share certain neural pathways. Clearly the difficulties experienced by the dyslexic musician are complex. However, providing help is not as difficult as it may first appear. To be effective, tuition must be embedded in an understanding of metacognition, enabling the student to develop their own toolbox of strategies and ultimately opening the door to independence for the student.

# Supporting Children with Dyslexia: Lessons from 'Every Child Matters'

Sheena Bell

A few years ago a key green paper emerged from a government rocked by scandals involving the repeated failure of agencies to link up their care for children at risk: ECM (Every Child Matters) (DfES 2003). This was followed up by legislation in the Children Act (2004), a far-reaching act which, it has been suggested, may take a generation to fully implement (Reid 2005). Although it is unclear how the newly elected coalition government in 2010 will move this agenda forward, ECM has already required education, health and social care authorities to organise closer links to provide a service that will cover all aspects of a child's development.

Whatever the future holds, the ECM programme still provides a useful framework for mapping the support of children with dyslexia. As any dyslexia teacher or supporter knows, dyslexia involves a range of difficulties which can have far-reaching consequences on the life-chances of children. Even throughout adulthood, well after basic literacy skills have been mastered, the marks made by dyslexia can continue affecting the well-being of individuals and their chances of achieving their potential (Bell 2010).

Successful dyslexia teaching should ensure that the aims of ECM are embedded in programmes. Specialist teachers and assessors share the responsibility for maximising the possibility of every child with dyslexia realising their full potential in education and in society. Specialists should be equipped to develop and extend the competences of other teachers and professionals in Local Authorities, by providing training opportunities and informing the procurement and development of teaching materials. This chapter takes the strands of ECM and suggests ways of mapping them to the dyslexia teaching agenda.

## ECM: Being Healthy

Children with dyslexia may be particularly susceptible to issues of self-esteem, often related to their achievement at school. This can lead to mental health difficulties at school or in later life. Teaching programmes must take into account students' emotional and affective needs; assessments for dyslexia must take health needs into consideration. Acquiring the mechanics of reading is important, but as a means to an end. Not only an improvement in reading, but also the relief that can be felt by a child who no longer considers himself as 'stupid', are important parts of a teaching programme. Although the key identifying factor of dyslexia is word-level literacy, dyslexia support is not simply about single word decoding. Children need to develop the metacognitive skills needed to maximise their strengths; only then can they begin to overcome the feeling of inferiority stemming from the gradual falling behind their peers.

More directly, these pupils may not have the literacy and numeracy skills to access health care and information. Programmes of support should link with the current needs of the learner both at school and in the wider environment. Adolescents, for example, may need to access information on contraception and drugs (both legal and illegal) in order to have a chance, equal to their peers, of staying healthy both mentally and physically.

## ECM: Staying Safe

Pupils with dyslexia may have associated difficulties with skills needed to stay safe. For example, they may not be able to remember names, appointments or directions, read timetables, safety notices and warnings and perform other everyday tasks. These can impact on safety as they are coping skills necessary for everyday life. Working memory difficulties could result in these children being unable to follow lists of instructions which could have dangerous results, for example, losing their way on an errand or conducting a scientific experiment in the wrong order. In addition, lack of literacy and maths skills may leave them vulnerable in different ways. For example, an inability to use higher-level reading skills may lead to exploitation through social networking sites on the internet and cyber-bullying. Assessment for teaching programmes and diagnostic reports must include informal information on the range of skills appropriate to the current needs of the learner.

## ECM: Enjoying and Achieving

Pupils with dyslexia often suffer as their difficulties in literacy skills may impede access to the whole curriculum. Barriers to learning may prevent them demonstrating competence in examinations, through difficulties of processing information. Rose (2009) highlights the importance of self-esteem with these children. Teachers should assess for dyslexic strengths as well as weaknesses ensuring that support programmes not only equip pupils to access the curriculum but also build on and celebrate their competences. Programme planning should take into consideration a child's need for enjoyment. Many children with dyslexia enjoy school subjects which do not involve literacy, participating enthusiastically in lessons such as sports, dance and art. However, it is tempting to deprive children of these lessons to fit in extra support, which may be discouraging and counterproductive ultimately. Similarly, a child who has struggled all day at school with reading and writing may gain more from pursuing hobbies and activities which reinforce their social skills and give feelings of satisfaction and achievement, rather than carrying on battling with homework. It is important for adults to be enthusiastic about helping a child improve their literacy skills, but a balance is needed.

## ECM: Making a Positive Contribution

Learning programmes should encourage and enable pupils with dyslexia to make use of their strengths to make a positive contribution to their schools and the wider community. It is widely accepted that children with dyslexia have many particular strengths, possibly linked to their learning differences or developed as compensatory factors, which are valuable assets to them both as learners and members of society. This diversity should be recognised and celebrated. For example, older pupils who have particular competences such as good oral or graphic presentation skills could be asked to present their work in this way rather than written form.

## ECM: Achieving Economic Well-being

Pupils with dyslexia may be at a disadvantage in a competitive employment market because of a failure to acquire the literacy skills necessary to acquire accreditation for their competences. Teachers must take this into consideration when planning programmes of support, as their advocacy and intervention may be needed to ensure that these children have a chance to show their knowledge in written examinations and access arrangement should be put in place where appropriate. In addition, the genetic links of dyslexia may be an indicator that parents of pupils with dyslexia may themselves have been disadvantaged in the employment market and, therefore, are not employed in high-earning professions, involving a cycle of social exclusion and poverty.

Every effort should be made to ensure that pupils are given a chance to communicate their needs and perceptions of their learning and that this is used in planning programmes. The implications and significance of diagnostic dyslexia reports should be discussed with learners at any age, to engage them in the learning process.

## Every Child with Dyslexia Matters

In conclusion, ECM still has lessons for those involved in dyslexia support. The most important expert on a child's needs is the child himself and so teachers must develop skills in listening to the views of their pupils. Taking careful consideration of the voices of children with dyslexia demands consultation with pupils at all stages of the teaching and assessment process. Communication with learners and parents or carers throughout the teaching and assessment process, carefully noting their views and responses, is vital if support is to be effective; teaching is not something to be applied in the same way as a medical cure. Framing dyslexia support with ECM reminds us that every child with dyslexia matters and we are responsible for taking a holistic perspective view of their needs.

## References

DfES (Department for Education and Skills) (2003) *Every Child Matters*. London, The Stationery Office.

Reid, K. (2005) The Implications of Every Child Matters and the Children Act for Schools. *Pastoral Care in Education.* 23, 12–18.

Bell, S. (2010) Inclusion for Adults with Dyslexia: Examining the Transition Periods of a Group of Adults in England: *'Clever is when you have come to a brick wall and you have got to get over it without a ladder.'* JORSEN Available online.

# New Developments

# Dyslexia/SpLD Professional Development Framework

Catherine Carroll

## Background

Over the past decade there has been a steady increase in the number of professionals within a range of educational settings who have sought to increase and develop their knowledge and

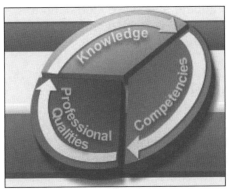

expertise in the teaching and support of pupils with dyslexia/SpLD. At the same time, the development of more inclusive settings and inclusive teaching has meant that all professionals are required to be able to deliver a curriculum that provides an effective education for all learners. In order to support this development, there has been a corresponding proliferation of different methods and routes through which the required knowledge and skills can be acquired. These include qualifications at undergraduate and post graduate levels, short courses and various other continuing professional development (CPD) opportunities. One consequence of this expansion has been that it can be somewhat confusing to a professional new and not so new to the field, as to the level of knowledge and skills needed for specific roles and what might be the best way to acquire the required level of competence. In order to help clarify this current situation and contribute to the implementation of some of the recommendations from the Rose Review, the Dyslexia SpLD Trust was commissioned to write a Framework for Best Practices.

The writing of the Framework began in November 2009 and from the very start of the project, one of the aims was to ensure that a wide variety of stakeholders working in different settings and with a wealth of knowledge and expertise in the area of dyslexia/SpLD were invited to take part and contribute to the process of developing the structure and content of the framework. The stakeholders included representatives from the Department of Education, National Strategies, the Training and Development Agency for schools, Local Authorities (LA), universities, non-governmental organisations and training providers. A conference was held in March 2010 where participants were invited to contribute and share ideas and this was followed up with a series of meetings with a smaller focus group to shape the final Framework.

Whilst considering the dyslexia/SpLD content of the Framework, it was recognised by those involved in the planning process, that for the Framework to be more effective it had to be compatible with and support, other related frameworks and the wider inclusion policy context. Consequently, various other frameworks such as the Qualifications and Credit Framework, the Professional Standards for Teachers, the Speech, Language and Communication Framework, the Inclusion Development Programme, to name just a few examples, also informed the content of the Framework.

## Aims

For the first time within the field, the Framework will encompass the levels of knowledge and skills required to fulfill various roles across the workforce to support learners with dyslexia/SpLD. The Framework will serve as a reference point in the creation and implementation of coherent and appropriate training and professional development across the education workforce. In doing so it will bring the following benefits to professionals, learners with dyslexia/SpLD and their families:

- Provide a simple and straightforward route map defining the knowledge and skills required at various levels and career points.

- Allow individuals within the education profession to identify and evaluate their training needs and those professionals with wider CPD responsibilities such as members of school leadership teams, governors and LAs to identify, deliver and evaluate CPD.

- Provide guidance for the mapping and development of a range of qualifications to support learners with dyslexia/SpLD.

- Encourage clear academic and professional progression routes from initial qualification to post graduate level, for the workforce involved in supporting learners with dyslexia.

- Provide a common focus for organisations who are commissioning training programmes so that they appropriately address the specifically identified knowledge, understanding and skills as indicated through the framework.

---

### Dyslexia-SpLD Trust Professional Development Framework

**About**

The Dyslexia/SpLD Professional Development Framework is an easy to use online tool that encompasses the levels of knowledge and skills required across the education workforce to support all learners with dyslexia/SpLD.

(+) About the Framework

(+) What are the benefits of using the Framework?

(+) How was the Framework developed?

(+) Start a self assessment

## Content

Although, at time of going to press, the Framework is currently at the pilot stage it is envisaged that the Framework will be available to be completed on line and via the Dyslexia/SpLD Trust website. The knowledge and skills within the Framework will be presented around six main strands, as identified in Figure 1: A, B, C, D, E and F.

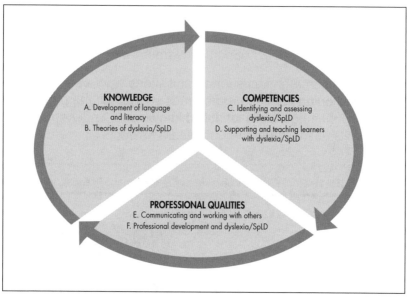

**Figure 1 Dyslexia/SpLD Framework for Best Practices – Strands**

For each strand individual competencies are allocated to one of five progressive stages of knowledge and levels of skill which correspond to specific roles across the workforce such as a teaching assistant, a Special Educational Needs Coordinator / Inclusion Manager or those professionals working in specialist and advisory roles working across many educational settings.

When first completing the Framework, an individual is requested to select the stage which is most appropriate to their role and from there they are presented with a number of statements from which they assess their individual level of knowledge and/ or skill against the competency using a grading system. After completing the Framework, the individual is presented with a report that identifies strengths and those areas that might be a focus for further training and development. There will also be a link to suggestions for resources that could support the development of a particular skill or area of knowledge.

## Project Timeline

As previously mentioned, the Framework is currently in the pilot stage. A number of different professionals will be asked to complete the pilot Framework and a survey or interview to provide feedback on a range of aspects including accessibility, relevancy and quality of feedback and comments on the potential of the Framework to provide a focus and source for further professional development. For professionals with management and CPD responsibilities, feedback will include how the Framework might be used to inform specific roles, responsibilities and appraisal processes. For providers of CPD, training and qualifications, feedback will be sought as to how the Framework provides a reference for informing the content and level of training they deliver. It is planned that the findings of the pilot will be completed by January 2011 with the final Framework completed by March 2011. For the Framework to then be released nationally, funding will need to be secured to ensure this process. Please check the Dyslexia/SpLD Trust website for further developments.

Finally, the members of the steering group would like to thank all the stakeholders and members of the focus group who have contributed so valuably to the process of writing the framework to date.

# What is SASC? SpLD Assessment Standards Committee [SASC]

Lynn Greenwold

In recent years the demand for diagnostic assessments of specific learning difficulties has grown considerably. Assessments are increasingly needed for specific purposes such as determining the right to Access Arrangements in examinations and the eligibility for the Disabled Students' Allowances in higher education. As the demand for assessments has grown, more professionals with qualifications in assessment of specific learning difficulties either as psychologists or as specialist teachers have become involved in this field. As a result of this, pressure for effective monitoring of standards in assessment has grown – both from those bodies such as the Department for Education, the Joint Council or the Student Loans Company who use assessment reports to make important decisions and from within the professions themselves.

The Department for Education and Skills was responsible for setting up a working group to consider the whole question of assessments for eligibility for the Disabled Students' Allowances. This working group produced useful guidance on procedures, the choice of tests and the format of assessment reports for this particular purpose. In addition, the working group recognised and emphasised in its report the need for some means of monitoring the quality of assessments, not on a case-by-case basis, but by ensuring that assessments were carried out by people who possessed requisite knowledge and skills to do the job to the highest professional standards. The quality of an assessment and subsequent report depends primarily on the knowledge and skills of the assessor rather than the selection of tests used. It is from this set of circumstances that the impetus has come for a Practising Certificate in Assessment which:

- Encourages continuing professional development in the skills of assessment.

- Recognises and awards these skills.

- Is valid for a set period of time only and then will need to be renewed.

SASC, the SpLD Assessment Standards Committee grew out of that Working Party and was established as a standard-setting group concerned with the diagnostic assessment of specific learning difficulties in an educational setting. SASC seeks to extend the principles of good practice contained in the Guidelines across all ag e ranges and throughout the profession.

This group also encompasses the SpLD Test Evaluation Committee [STEC] which serves to evaluate test tools and, drawing on expertise across the sector, maintain a list of approved testing tools for SpLDs in higher education.

## New CPD Authorisation Scheme

To further underpin standards in Continuing Professional Development, SASC is introducing an authorisation scheme for the continuing professional development of specialist teachers and other professionals engaged in the diagnostic assessment of Specific Learning Difficulties.

From 2012 there is a new requirement that a minimum of five hours of this CPD must be delivered by SASC-authorised providers.

In March 2010 SASC launched its new website enabling CPD providers to apply online to become SASC authorised and have their CPD provision listed on the new site. SASC has developed this new Authorisation Scheme and website in response to the recommendations of the DfES SpLD Working Group 2005. The new website will be an important source of information and is likely to become the first port of call for those professionals who are looking for suitable CPD training courses delivered by SASC-authorised providers to meet their CPD needs.

The launch of this new website is an opportunity for training providers to design and develop CPD courses that will meet the needs of specialist assessors. It also provides an opportunity for training providers to apply to become recognised as SASC-authorised CPD providers in time to benefit those assessors who are building their CPD evidence for the renewal of their Assessment Practising Certificates in 2012 and beyond.

If you would like to know more, visit the SASC website or contact SASC at:

**SASC**

PO Box 10
Evesham
Worcs
WR11 1ZW

Tel:    01386 712740
Fax:    01386 712716
**info@sasc.org.uk**

# Further and
# Higher Education

# Supporting Art Students in Higher Education

Fleur Campbell

'If a picture paints 1,000 words why write an essay?' Good question! If painting is the way that you express your thoughts and knowledge it can feel somewhat unfair and contradictory to be asked to use another medium. How would historians react to being told to paint a mural? The fact is most art undergraduates now face at least one significant piece of writing each semester.

You don't have to be an artist to support arts students but it can give an insight into their working methods. Creative people have a good idea of the 'end result' of their work before they start. They refer to this 'whole' constantly in their mind's eye; often without sketching or preparatory work. In contrast, the words 'write an essay of 5,000 words' can conjure up the daunting image of a huge and structured file of work.

Many dyslexics have a 'whole picture' style of working so for the *dyslexic art* student their brain has been working in this way for most of their life, thus they can be ill-equipped to put an ordered and sequential essay together. Their dyslexia may have caused a weakness with sequence and moving from point to point in a methodical, left-brained way is beyond their experience. It is well documented that the dyslexic has great difficulty in transferring excellent verbal skills to paper. Given oral opportunities to display knowledge and understanding, they may well excel but the written form of language is rarely their preferred route.

Coupled with their intrinsic cognitive difficulties, creative art students will have spent their final school years taking practical exams – BTECs, NVQs or Art/Photography/Ceramics A levels – subjects which often offer alternative responses to the researched and constructed essays of more traditional subjects. The nature of dyslexia means that even if they have been taught to plan, write and proof read, without regular practice they will lose the skill; the familiar lack of automaticity rears its head.

The essay will not be the only written requirement as students will attend Contextual Studies lectures where note taking becomes necessary. Most dyslexics find listening to verbal information, processing the themes quickly enough to write them down, finding the right spelling and forming the correct letters overwhelming and usually not worth the valiant attempt.

Personal statements, reflective journals, diaries, applications for competitions and evaluations of tasks will all demand further literacy skills and these are just the writing aspects of the courses; reading poses yet another challenge.

Reading written briefs can be the most crucial skill of all, affecting a whole semester's work. These briefs will often be written in an academic way to stimulate and provoke the intellect and creativity, yet a dyslexic student will often look for the shortest sentence with the smallest words in the hope that this will be the simplest to interpret. This does them a disservice – if given the information verbally, with plenty of time to repeat and consider the content – they may well choose a far more complex challenge.

Supporting the dyslexic art student involves sensitivity, practical solutions and a positive attitude. Many students will not have been diagnosed until they reach university and will have 'coped' until the demands of the curriculum prove too much. Others may have relied on a great deal of support in school and will feel lost without the constant reminders and reassurance. Some are embarrassed by their dyslexia, although public opinion is now very positive due to the list of well-known successful dyslexics in so many artistic fields.

Many dyslexics have difficulty with organisation and it can be a huge relief for an intelligent, independent student to be reassured that they are 'typical' rather than 'abnormal' with this difficulty. Teaching strategies for planning and breaking down projects into small manageable bites is essential for well-being and productivity. Working backwards from deadlines will show how time can be divided up; working through an essay plan shows how the writing can be broken into small chunks; discussing titles to evaluate how much the student already knows will help determine the time needed for research.

Structuring can be a minefield. Choosing and interpreting questions, researching sufficiently, finding quotes/illustrations, making notes, making a plan, writing cohesively, spelling accurately, proof reading and keeping to a deadline all challenge their weakest areas.

Directing students towards a title that reflects something of their own working practice gives a good start. Discussing what is already known highlights what needs to be researched. Planning (mind map, bullet points, headings) will give instant structure. Allocating an appropriate word count to each section and tackling one at a time is less daunting. Inserting quotes will start the word count and give further structure. Remind students about the 'undo' button! This encourages brainstorming which can then be edited. Reading the essay aloud will help with proof reading and style.

Time management presents problems for many. Dyslexics often leave tasks too late and then either ignore them or panic! Alarms can be set on mobile phones and computers to remind them of lectures, meetings, 'hand in' days, etc. Encourage the use of notebooks and diaries to be kept – in duplicate at least! The weekly chat with the dyslexia tutor is often cited by students as the most positive aspect of the support on offer at university. The meeting allows for consolidation of previous learning and the opportunity to set small, achievable tasks for next time. Study skills can be taught and followed up – frequently through practical application during the week's lectures, seminars, workshops, gallery visits, project meetings etc.

Inevitably essays prove the biggest challenge; often due to the research requirement. Capitalise on a student's preferred learning style to make the first step easier – discuss the title with an auditory learner, use illustrations of the initial ideas for a visual learner or make a mind map with a kinaesthetic student. A lot of research will involve books, journals or websites – teach the student to use skimming and scanning techniques to maximise this experience. Often reading a chapter summary or the 'topic sentence' of a lengthy paragraph will deliver sufficient information without wading through a complex text.

A 'browse aloud' function on the computer enables one to listen to an article being read. Weak readers find recordings of 'interviews' with artists or film makers offer a comfortable way of accessing relevant information. Those with visual weakness may find a coloured overlay (usually blue for this age group) can be helpful, as can altering the background colour of their computer screen to suit them.

Practical ways of storing research include colour-coded folders for printed information/handouts/press cuttings etc.; using a dictaphone for inspired thoughts or to interview others. The essay structure can be formatted into a word document with headings for introduction, paragraphs and conclusion – brief phrases, keywords etc. can then be typed in as they occur and linked at a later stage. A tutor can help by scribing initial thoughts if typing skills are poor and students can be encouraged to use a speech-to-text software – Dragon Naturally Speaking v10 is good.

For dyslexic art students in particular the 'mind map' gives an invaluable overview of the task on one page – better still if enhanced by colour and image. 'Inspirations' software provides an excellent on-screen version which can be moved around or ordered into lists and paragraphs. Actually, this can be done just as satisfactorily with pieces of A1 paper and lots of Post-its! Post-its are a great analogy for the small 'bits' that make up the project and can be a reassuring starting point…anyone can think of a word or two for that first Post-it.

It is vital to reinforce the student's belief in their ability to deliver their opinions and knowledge in written form. Maintaining a positive attitude is a great strength of dyslexics – they are ideas people and when one idea fails they come up with something else.

However, these talented students struggle to use their underlying abilities to generate well-researched, well-written material. Our role as tutors is to use our talents to support, mentor and train a student in acquiring the skills and independence to demonstrate their knowledge and opinions in their written assignments. Doing this at university stands them in good stead for future careers.

# Screening for Dyscalculia: Development and Delivery

Claire Trott

## Introduction

DyscalculiUM is a new first-line screening tool to identify students who may be at risk of dyscalculia. The name and capitalisation derives from the key focus of the tool, that of understanding mathematics (UM). It has been developed over a number of years by Trott and Beacham at Loughborough University and follows extensive research and development.

## Background

The conceptual understanding of number is one of the main features in the definition of dyscalculia from The National Numeracy Strategy (DfES, 2001, page 2): "Dyscalculia is a condition that affects the ability to acquire arithmetical skills. Dyscalculic learners may have difficulty understanding simple number concepts, lack an intuitive grasp of numbers and have problems learning number facts and procedures. Even if they produce a correct answer or use a correct method, they may do so mechanically and without confidence." Understanding is also emphasised by Chinn (2006, page 16): "A lack of a true comprehension or understanding of maths will be a key characteristic of dyscalculic people". Furthermore, the primary statement in The National Numeracy Strategy definition is 'the ability to acquire arithmetical skills', which serves to highlight acquisition rather than the mechanical procedures of arithmetic. Butterworth (1999) contends that numbers are conceived as a numerosity or a collection of items. "An intuitive grasp of number" would imply comparisons of these quantities and therefore an understanding of the inter-relationships between numbers. These, together with possible inferences, are also central to screening for dyscalculia.

There are various reasons why mathematical difficulties occur: dyscalculia, knowledge gaps, poor teaching or long periods of absence as well as other neurodiversities. "It is important to make a clear distinction between students whose mathematical difficulties are due to dyslexia or other neurodiversities and those who struggle with mathematics as a result of dyscalculia (Trott, 2010, page 19)". The learning of number facts and procedures, as specified in the National Numeracy Strategy definition above, involves rote learning and recall and is known to be an 'at risk' area for those with dyslexia and other neurodiverse profiles.

## The Model

The model that was developed, in parallel with the screener, is given in Figure 2.

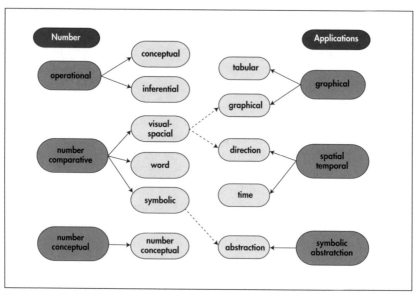

**Figure 2: The Model For Dyscalculium: A First-Line Screening Tool**

It is built on the three key areas essential to understanding number: number concepts, quantitative comparisons (subdivided into items that employ words, symbols and visual spatial representations) and operations. The latter being further split into conceptual understanding of operations and the making of inferences from given results, as illustrated by the exemplar item in figure 3:

---

Which sum gives the larger answer?
Select the correct answer

**Sum A 2458 + 327**

**Sum B 2456 + 326**

  ○ Sum A
  ○ Sum B
  ○ Both the same
  ○ Cannot tell

---

**Figure 3: An Exemplar Item from Dyscalculium**

"The screening tool also includes several applications of these key elements, thus helping to identify what is conceptually understood and what can be effectively applied" Trott (2010). These applications focus on understanding graphs and tables, directions, time and symbolic notation. Numerical understanding incorporates inductive reasoning, visualisation and quantitative skill. It is a logical analysis of visual symbolic information. These elements are blended together within the core elements of the screening tool.

## Development

Very encouraging results were obtained from the early trials of DysCalculiUM (Beacham and Trott, 2005, 2006). From the outset, the appearance of the screening tool and the use of language were key considerations. There is no set time limit within which the student is required to complete the test. This is designed to reduce the pressure it causes and thereby the implicit anxiety. For those who struggle with understanding mathematics, there is frequently a severe attendant issue of mathematical confidence. Without the timing, it is possible to establish what the participant understands, rather than what can be achieved under the pressure of time constraints. However, participants are encouraged to move forward through the items in the screener and not to dwell on them for too long. Following the early trials, modifications were made to both the items in the screener and its appearance. All of the items had to fit in one screen shot so that scrolling is not necessary. Consideration was also given to the background colour in order to reduce the visual stress.

As noted earlier, mathematical difficulties can be a consequence of many factors, including dyslexia or other neurodiversities such as dyspraxia, particularly with regard to working memory, processing speed and language. Thus, it has always been a priority for the screener to differentiate the dyscalculic student from the dyslexic student. Throughout the development and trials, measures of sensitivity and specificity were used to compare three groups. These were a dyscalculic group (those with a recognised assessment of dyscalculia) with a dyslexic group (those with a recognised assessment of dyslexia) and a control group (those with no known neurodiverse profile). It was important to effectively distinguish the dyscalculic group from the other two groups. An exemplar item will serve to illustrate this: Figures 4 and 5 show the items together with the percentage of each group achieving the correct response. These results are taken from one of the trials. The items ask participants to select the larger of two given numbers. The first shows good discrimination between the dyscalculic group and the other two groups, as required for successful screening. In order to answer this item correctly, the participant must understand the concept of decimal place value. The second does not show the required differentiation and a correct response can be obtained without understanding decimal place value. The reversal in the digits appears to have presented difficulties for the dyslexic group. This second item was therefore removed from the screener.

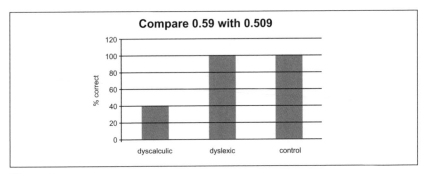

**Figure 4**

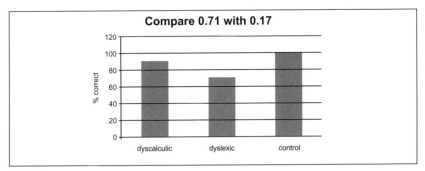

**Figure 5**

Development of the screener continued through further trials and modifications, including trials on a much larger scale that collected general data for the Further and Higher Education population (n=504) so that 'severely at risk' and 'at risk' thresholds could be established. These were accordingly set at the 2nd and 8th percentile ranks. Furthermore, the screener was trialled on a number of students who had already been identified as dyscalculic through recognised assessments. "The overall picture of results gives substantial evidence in support of the effectiveness of the DysCalculiUM screening tool, not least in the substantial agreement between the appropriate indicators of 'at risk' performance on the screener and those individual students who have already been identified as dyscalculic through recognised assessments" (Trott, 2009, page 134).

## DysCalculiUM: The Profiler

The 11 sub-categories from the model given in Figure 2, provides the basis for an individual profile that shows the areas of relative strength and weakness, in addition to an overall 'at risk' indicator. The profile report from the DysCalculiUM screening profile can act as a useful starting point for subsequent one-to-one learning support. An exemplar profile is given in Figure 6. This shows an overall score that indicated 'severely at risk of dyscalculia'. The profile provides further evidence for this, with 7 highlighted categories. The profile suggested a difficulty in understanding number concepts and making numerical comparisons between numbers. This is likely to impact upon understanding the concept of number operations and in making inferences from them. However, no difficulties with graphical and tabular information, time and spatial directions were apparent. These are more visual areas and suggest a visual learner.

| | Severely at risk | At risk | Not at risk |
|---|---|---|---|
| **OVERALL SCORE** | ■ | | |
| | | | |
| No. Conceptual | | ■ | |
| No. Comparative: Word | | ■ | |
| No. Comparative: Symbol | ■ | | |
| No. Comparative: Vis-Sp | ■ | | |
| Graphical | | | ■ |
| Tabular | | | ■ |
| Symbolic Abstraction | ■ | | |
| Spatial Direction | | | ■ |
| Time | | | ■ |
| Operational: Conceptual | ■ | | |
| Operational: Inferential | ■ | | |

Figure 6: Profile from DysCalcuiUM

## Delivery

DysCalculiUM will be an online screener for dyscalculia. The learner accesses the DysCalculiUM portal and completes the screener. The results are automatically analysed. The tutor can then access the portal, review the results and profiles and identify those who are 'at risk' and require further investigation.

## Conclusion

Our understanding of dyscalculia is many years behind that of dyslexia. However, by building on our growing knowledge of how mathematics is conceived and understood, it is hoped the DysCalculiUM first-line screening tool will provide a much needed step in the identification process and a platform for subsequent learning support for those who struggle at the conceptual level of mathematical thinking.

*DysCalculiUM: A First-Line Screening Tool for Dyscalculia* will be available from Iansyst Ltd., Cambridge in Autumn 2010

## References

Beacham N. and Trott C. (2006) *Project Report: Wider Use of Dyscalculium, an Electronic Tool for Dyscalculia In H.E.* MSOR Connections Vol. 6(2) pp 12-19

Beacham N. and Trott C. (2005) *Development of a First-Line Screener for Dyscalculia in Higher Education,* The Skill Journal, 81, pp 13-19

Butterworth, B. (1999) *The Mathematical Brain*. London: Macmillan.

Chinn S. (2006) *What Dyslexia can tell us about Dyscalculia,* Dyslexia Review Vol. 18 (1), pp 15-17

DfES. (2001), The National Numeracy Strategy, *Guidance to Support Pupils with Dyslexia and Dyscalculia,* DfES 0512/2001 **http://publications.teachernet.gov.uk/ eOrderingDownload/DfES-0512-2001.pdf** (accessed 26/08/10)

Trott, C. (2010), *Dyscalculia: A Practitioner's View*, Assessment and Development Matters.", British Psychology Society, 2(2), pp. 19-21.

Trott, C. (2009), *Dyscalculia,* in Pollak D (ed) Neurodiversity in Higher Education: Positive Responses to Specific Learning Differences, Wiley and Son, Chichester, pp. 125-148.

# Why are Boys More Reticent than Girls to Accept Help for their Specific Learning Difficulties?

Vicki McNicol

Over the past eighteen months, in my role as a disability student allowance assessor, I have assessed a considerable number of university students with dyslexia making recommendations on their behalf to enable them to gain a grant to cover the cost of assistive technology and learning support to enable them to cope with the demands of higher education.

I could not help but notice how female students readily agree with my recommendations for an hour's learning support a week to enable them to receive specialist dyslexia tuition. However, the male students need cajoling. It is true to say that the more confident young men found the suggestion of additional learning support a more acceptable proposition.

This anomaly has caused me to question why is it that some young men need persuading to engage in a process that ultimately will help them to learn new approaches to cope with their academic studies. Take Aiden for example. He is a student reading for a degree in Graphic Design. He gained eight GCSEs grades A – D and went on to achieve a BTech National Diploma in Art and Design, which enabled him to gain a place at university. During his first year as an undergraduate he was referred for dyslexia screening and then a diagnostic assessment, which confirmed that he is moderately dyslexic with high average general ability. This was not recognised during his school career. Aiden recalled struggling to develop literacy skills in primary school. He was given additional support in the classroom from a teaching assistant. His parents suspected that something was not quite right as Aiden was articulate and appeared intelligent through his interests and ability to discuss them. Aiden was a popular child having many friends. His parents had noticed that Aiden frequently failed to follow instructions forgetting what he had been asked to do. Aiden's teachers consistently commented that he was an inattentive child, often distracting those around him in the classroom with idle chatter and he had a tendency not to complete classroom activities. Aiden's attainment in reading, writing and mathematics was two years below his age-peers. In discussion with Aiden, I recognised that his dismissive attitude towards additional learning support at university directly correlated with his experiences at school.

Like many of the students I see, Aiden had lost the will to overcome his learning difficulties and believed trying to overcome them was futile. These young men are prepared to give up their aspirations and settle for careers that they believe they are fit for. Their choice of degree courses are based on that they will only have twenty-five percent of written work to tackle, the rest of their studies being practical and also the fact that there are no examinations. They appear to overlook the fact that the written element of the course requires in-depth research and a good standard of academic essays. This accounts for the reason why I assess so many young men in the second and third years of their degree course.

Young women appear to be very keen at the start of their academic careers to obtain as much support as they can. They are more open to learning new study strategies and their determination to tackle their learning difficulties is apparent. Their difference in attitude is striking as they see the degree course as a medium to achieve their aspirations rather than settling for something that is less than they desire.

Is it that young women are more resilient, enabling them to cope better with negative learning experiences? Are they more creative in their thinking which enables them to see that they are able to take a different path towards their chosen careers? Their determination to succeed is almost tangible.

I can't help but wonder if the answer lies in the different ways in which we nurture boys and girls. Are our expectations for boys to achieve too high? Or is it because the ethos of removing competition in our schools has militated against boys becoming emotionally robust?

I actually believe that it is more to do with the different rates of maturity in males and females, which impacts on each gender's ability to cope with negative criticism. I also believe that from an early age girls are becoming much more aware of how to deal with their flaws. Learning support, therefore, is just another tool in their make-up box that will enable them to become who they aspire to be, just like wearing the appropriate coloured lip stick to flatter their skin tone.

The young men I assess also appear to have a sense that receiving learning support is somehow cheating, whereas using assistive technology is more acceptable. Perhaps this is because the use of assistive technology is more discreet? Or is it that technology per se is so widely used that assistive technology is more acceptable?

One thing I know for sure is that when I point out that specialist learning support will help them to overcome their difficulties not only in an educational setting but also in the workplace, the young men I assess become more open to the suggestion. I explain that learning what strengths they have and learning how to utilise their strengths to overcome their weaknesses will enable them to take control of their dyslexia. It will help them in all aspects of their lives as it will help them to avoid repeated failure and reshape the way they approach new situations. It will allow their innate ability to shine through enabling them to demonstrate what they can do, liberating their true potential. I encourage them to at least try it for six weeks and see for themselves what difference it can make, after which they can decide whether or not to continue. In my experience very few students decide to stop once they have achieved some progress in an area that hitherto was a stumbling block.

Parents should not underestimate their influence on their son's attitude to receiving additional learning support. Approaching this subject needs to be done sensitively as a heavy handed approach could be received as additional pressure. I have noted many young men who have felt failure through not living up to their perceived parents' expectations. Parents might approach this subject through identifying their sons' aspirations and pointing out their qualities that help them to believe that their aspirations are achievable. I have observed how feelings of self belief can be boosted by the power of a parent's confidence in his child's ability to achieve goals. I have seen the power of suggestion that something is possible transform the way in which a young person perceives himself, helping him to reshape his aspirations. If learning support is spoken of in positive terms and seen to be an opportunity to gain life changing skills – through teaching methods that bear no resemblance to those received in the past – then young men may be less reticent in accepting this form of support. Any discussion on this matter should be broached in an affirmation of possibility and potential to raise the self esteem of their sons empowering them to accept the vital help they need to reach their goals.

Association of Dyslexia Specialists in Higher Education

The Association of Dyslexia Specialists in Higher Education (ADSHE) was set up to share knowledge and inform good practice in working with students with dyslexia, dyspraxia and other SpLDs in Higher Education.

ADSHE aims to:

- *Work towards establishing parity of provision so these students will be assured of appropriate support throughout the HE sector*
- *Establish commonly accepted codes of good practice*
- *Allow members to share experiences and overcome feelings of isolation*
- *Provide CPD for members*

ADSHE has expanded its influence significantly and now has an active role in addressing relevant issues at a national level.

There are eight regional groups which meet regularly throughout the year and general meetings are held in London four times a year.

The annual ADSHE Networking Day is a popular and informative event.

If you are working with students in Higher Education please get in touch by going to our website **www.adshe.org.uk** or emailing our administrator on **adshedyslexia@yahoo.co.uk**

# Training and Support in the Further Education/Higher Education FE/HE Sectors

Francis Bloom

As greater numbers of dyslexic learners reach the FE/HE sectors, the need for well-trained supporters becomes ever more important. As their needs go beyond literacy in many cases, the focus of support must be at higher order skills. I draw on experience of training in an FE college in a multi-ethnic outer London Borough and from discussion with colleagues in other FE/HE establishments.

## FE   The Issues

### The Right Course:

This is crucial to a successful outcome. At enrolment during interview this issue must be assessed through questioning previous achievements and areas of difficulty. The difficulties in FE may be literacy based and Access courses generally allow for this. However, those students on A level or equivalent courses will have functional though uneven skills in literacy.

### The Supporters:

What route have they come from? What are their expectations/ understanding of the job? What training/skills do they bring to the job? The gamut runs from well-intentioned persons with spare time who wish to help in their community to qualified special needs trained teachers. In between there are a myriad of gradations. It is the responsibility of the FE establishment and most likely the Head of the Learning Development Department (which may have many alternative names) to ensure that their personnel receive training where it is needed.

## The Nomenclature:

Tutor Assistants (TA), Tutor Support (TS), Teaching Assistants (TA), Learning Assistants (LA), Learning Support Assistants (LSA), Learning Advisors (LA). Acronyms galore!

It may be that the learning advisor has come from a position of good knowledge and experience and has solid understanding of the theory and practice of working in the dyslexia field. However, this title can be used for staff who have 'picked up' the basics of literacy support, with little or no training. They may be paid half the money for half the skills. These staff are intended to be working under the aegis of a trained lead member of staff with responsibility to supervise the advisor. In practice in a busy FE college the timing may not work out well and the little-trained learning advisor is left to his, or more often her, own devices relying, we hope, on good common sense to 'advise' the student how best to become an independent learner.

At the other end of the spectrum all the above titles can denote well-organised, hard-working staff, part of a structured hierarchy that reinforces both the supporters and the supported.

## The Students:

What route have they come from? What information on their learning needs has travelled with them? If they come directly from school and have a Statement of Educational Need then information should be available. But if enrolling at, for example, age 20+ it is likely that there will be no information other than that provided by the student.

## The Support:

Support should be targeted at producing independent learners. This requires the supporters to have a deep understanding of the memory, organisation and processing difficulties a dyslexic learner will be likely to have together with a thorough knowledge of compensatory strategies to assist the students. This should include the most current Reader IT aids. See **www.dyslexic. com/altformat-needed**

Students arrive with their own expectations of success and as trainers we have a huge responsibility to train support tutors to enable these learners to reach for and attain, their potentials.

There may be a dichotomy between the student and the supporter where a compromise must be reached. The student wants to hand in a piece of work to meet an imminent deadline where the support tutor wants to teach the student time management and essay planning. How easy to correct the spelling and grammar, add a few touches through questioning the student and the assignment is done! No independent strategy has been learned, but dependency has been strengthened.

## Training FE/HE Supporters – The Issues:

### Training Costs for FE Staff

Young People's Learning Agency (YPLA) is the funding agency for 16–19 year olds, the Skills Funding Agency (SFA) covers 19+ students, particularly now, money is short. Some colleges do not offer remission of teaching hours, making the rigorous training harder in terms of time management. There is a lack of good quality courses across the UK with quality trainers which leads to a postcode lottery. E-learning or distance learning courses can help to address this, however, this type of study does not suit everyone. The BDA holds a list of accredited courses. It is important to choose a course that is not exclusively primary based, OCR courses, for instance, are generic and cover all sectors of education. Following the recommendations in the Rose Report (2009) the TDA has some funding available for school-age learners, it would be great if that could be extended to post 16.

### Finding a Student with SpLD to Teach

Who is responsible for identifying the student? The enrolment process should help here. Queries elicit disclosure of any learning difficulties, tutors refer their students as the course progresses and difficulties become obvious. The student may self-refer, in this case s/he is likely to be motivated to embrace the help offered.

## Special Examination Arrangements

A student with a disability must be neither advantaged nor disadvantaged when compared with other students, this underpins any assistance which can be offered. All colleges and universities have procedures to address this issue, details are generally to be found on their websites.

## HE: The Issues

As above but with more pressure on the outcomes as the students are further along their chosen career path.

Dyslexic difficulties remain even when reading is compensated. Difficulty with memory and speed of processing remains an issue for compensated adult readers. This in turn has an effect on the following:

- Difficulty with memory for factual information affects the ability to use and retain information from lecture presentations.

- Dyslexic students will be at a disadvantage if note taking is the only option in lectures. *They need handouts, preferably in advance, so that the vocabulary is familiar.*

- Speed or mode of presentation of lectures. *Lecturers need to have raised awareness of the difficulties this might pose.*

- These difficulties affect a variety of areas related both to study and social interaction with peers. *Again, raised awareness and openness on the part of the student are necessary.*

- Note-taking skills which require divided attention amongst listening, processing, choosing salient points and writing. *Multitasking is hard for the dyslexic. IT solutions with lectures available on the web or university intranet.*

## Recommendations Good Practice

Students applying for places in FE/HE establishments should check the websites carefully for inclusion of special needs students. If that is difficult they should go to their enrolment armed with prepared questions about support, students should be open and disclose difficulties.

Capel Manor College, an FE Horticulture College in Enfield, Middlesex, provides a first interview with a vocational tutor at enrolment, where mental health, exclusion and dyslexia are some of the issues covered. A second interview is set up with support staff to ascertain needs and how these will affect their chosen studies. The parent/carer is involved where appropriate and support offered is monitored. Students attend a Summer School in August where the whole Learning Support Department closely observe and discuss students to ensure that the course offered is tenable. Offers made are conditional on mandatory support in some cases. They may be offered induction of half a day, following that, the student attends two hours per week for 4–6 weeks where the object is to encourage independence. During Summer School, behaviour and ability to relate to peers and staff is assessed.

All staff are required to attend four days CPD. Within that, Learning Support Staff cover barriers to learning, interview procedures/techniques, communications and listening skills. These procedures help to retain students who become successful graduates.

The upshot is that both the FE and HE sectors must have rigorous procedures in place to identify and support students and recognise the need for meticulous procedures to monitor well-trained supporters whose *raison d'etre* is to create independent learners.

# Dyspraxia and Higher Education: the Role of the Educational Practitioner

Janet Skinner and Julia Kender

Practitioners agree on the overlap between dyslexia and dyspraxia and an examination of these specific learning difficulties based on current levels of understanding of cognition and literacy development suggests many commonalities.

However, the causal pathways leading to literacy difficulties may vary. In dyslexia, difficulties in decoding letters to sounds or sounds to letters produce phonological deficits that may lead to weak literacy skills.

In dyspraxia the causal pathways stem from visual spatial or visual motor problems and may be associated with co-ordination issues that will be more pronounced in text processing, for example, locating information when reading or organising ideas when writing.

Students with dyspraxia have difficulties beyond literacy and interventions need to recognise organisational difficulties beyond linguistics and text processing. Students often find working in a laboratory quite challenging. Courses involving fieldwork or placements put students under pressure to organise and complete activities within a very strict timeframe. Some dyspraxic students will struggle with practical aspects such as measuring and drawing in the field.

Dyspraxia research is less robust than dyslexia research and leads to controversies ranging from debates over definitions and terminology to uncertainty as to whether dyspraxia is the legitimate concern of health or education practitioners. Whilst many strategies to assist with organisation and time management may appear similar, students with dyspraxia may require more reinforcement and opportunities for overlearning.

Uncertainty over the nature and assessment of a dyspraxic profile generates differences of opinion over the necessary qualifications of assessors and the design and execution of interventions.

Successful intervention relies on accurate assessment but this may be obscured in adults by the acquisition of compensatory strategies masking the individual's profile. Essentially, dyspraxia describes a difficulty with planning, doing or acting.

Traditionally, in describing dyspraxia much more emphasis has been placed on difficulties of co-ordination and execution and perceptual motor difficulties than on the impact on literacy and organisational skills required of academic activity.

In considering the characteristics of dyspraxia the emphasis has been on the identification of poor body awareness (proprioception) and eye-hand co-ordination leading to difficulties in integrating visual and auditory information and turning this information into motor output.

The accurate diagnosis of dyspraxia requires the presence of indicators throughout life and the recognition of indications before the development of compensating strategies and activities. In the absence of such longitudinal information the presenting profile may easily be mis-associated with dyspraxia.

A specialist teacher assessor needs to take account of both the physical and educational aspects of dyspraxia but educational practitioners should exercise caution in labelling without a full history. There are several excellent checklists available that may be used by medical and educational practitioners to gain information about past and present physical difficulties.

Multi-disciplinary assessment is the ideal but is not often practical. Educationists need to be clear about the purpose of the assessment. What are the primary presenting factors? Does the student need support for study or for daily living or for both?

Educationists may find it helpful to concentrate on the impact of dyspraxia on organisational, ideational and sequential functioning problems. However, without the contextualisation in the assessment of motor control and co-ordination, muscle tone and skeletal form, educational assessors can only begin to form an opinion based on responses from students to questions rather than clinical tests. They may also take into account secondary characteristics such as self-confidence and self-awareness and reach a conclusion of a *specific learning difficulty consistent with a dyspraxic profile* but this does not constitute a diagnosis of the physical disability that is dyspraxia.

## Differing Profiles

Academic environments may be challenging for dyspraxic students because of their novelty and the requirement to manage unfamiliar situations. Practitioners need to be aware that although some compensatory skills may be readily transferred, there are other areas where the transition may be more problematic. In some situations the requirements may simply be time; in the physical environment, although many have learned compensatory strategies they may still need additional time to plan and execute tasks.

For many adults, self-esteem in managing social situations is probably more important than motor co-ordination issues, which may well be compensated over a lifetime. A new physical environment may present many bewilderingly new challenges to those with particular sequencing and memory difficulties who find navigating around a large campus or multi-site institution difficult. Some students may request halls nearer to campus or full catering to minimise difficulties.

There may be issues with group work because of time and spatial problems, for example, the need to review the output and contributions of other participants that may all be in different formats. Similar difficulties may arise when using new technology. For example, the co-ordination involved in texting may require a longer period of time to achieve an acceptable result.

The unfamiliar social environment of higher education and new forms of peer and power relationships of higher education may be particularly demanding to dyspraxic students. This might mean that mentoring as well as academic support is required.

Adult learners who have extensive experience of independent living may not be able to translate it into an academic environment. Dyspraxic students may need continuing support in adjusting to the autonomy and organisation needs of student living because of their organisational difficulties and problems in prioritisation and time management.

Poor verbal expression is likely to present difficulties in social interactions and difficulties in remembering or following verbal instructions may be particularly challenging in induction periods and when interpreting assessment tasks.

Poor time management, slow reading speeds and difficulties in prioritisation make keeping up with the required level of reading problematic. Difficulties in prioritisation and decision making may call for support in module choice and assistance in understanding timetables. Problems in the structuring of ideas coupled with slow writing speeds may make written work difficult and the limited social skills tend to make additional support in group work and classroom presentations necessary.

## Practical Support

Dyspraxic students often require more support than other SpLD students as their needs are more complex. They might require practical support such as adjusted showers, catered halls, study buddies for field trips, help with drawing and writing tasks and library and laboratory assistants. Many organisation and time-management strategies are similar to those for dyslexic students, but educational practitioners need to respond to individual need. Sometimes strategies appear not to work as well or require more reinforcement. Dyspraxic students often require structured support, with templates, mind maps and support for essay planning and editing skills. They may need help tackling essay/exam questions or alternative forms of assessment. They might well require extra thinking time in seminars or presentations. Visual formats to support word retrieval difficulties or organising ideas as well as a range of memory techniques to aid weak working memory are often very useful. Some dyspraxic students would benefit from rehearsal modelling techniques or even role play in some situations such as preparation for group work or presentations.

Thus, the challenges for support staff lie in managing service provision in the context of wide-ranging individual differences.

# The Case for Study Skills Coaching

Liz Amesbury

The provision of study skills tuition for students with dyslexia and other specific learning difficulties is now widespread in the higher education sector. The role brings its own unique challenges, which are best explained in relation to the study demands of the sector, assessment requirements for higher education and the emotional distress experienced by dyslexic students. The study skills tutor role inevitably involves navigating these challenges and the solutions are not easily found in traditional approaches to teaching and learning. A common complaint amongst study skills tutors in higher education is that there is a lack of understanding about their role and the demands it involves. Their remit is to develop their students' study skills but it is often unrecognised that the complexity of working within the higher education sector extends beyond teaching strategies for study. Developing specialist coaching skills will enable tutors to facilitate change at deeper levels than study behaviour, enhancing their student's success as well as their own professional self-esteem and sense of expertise.

## Study Demands of the Sector

The nature of higher education means that a study skills tutor is presented with students from diverse programme areas, many of which are unrelated to their own area of expertise. This variance means that, for example, a tutor who is an arts graduate may be placed with a student studying a course with a predominantly scientific basis. There are elements of study skills that are generic, such as teaching students how to organise their learning resources, develop research skills and manage their time effectively so a tutor may be confident helping a student deal with these kinds of challenges.

However, each subject also brings its own unique demands that are highly specialised. Even within scientific report writing, the generic element is not easily decipherable and is often overridden by the unique requirements of individual topics. A student attending study skills tuition has the expectation that their tutor's role is to support in understanding and producing coursework. Clearly there are boundaries and the content and written expression must be the student's own. However, a study skills tutor who is a science graduate could maintain these boundaries whilst supporting the student with the production of a scientific report, whereas an arts graduate tutor would find this difficult.

When faced with study demands that are outside their own area of expertise, tutors may feel inadequate about their capabilities and unsure whether they are meeting the requirements of their role. They somehow need to navigate such minefields whilst maintaining rapport with their students and satisfying themselves that their limitations are justifiable. Developing a sufficient level of expertise to support students from diverse subject areas would require significant investment in additional training for tutors. Unfortunately, higher education study skills tutors are often employed on a freelance basis or by external agencies and lack sufficient line management support, training opportunities and integration with their professional colleagues.

## Assessment Requirements for Higher Education

For many years, study skills requirements for higher education were finite and predictable. A range of essay formats and written examinations formed a significant part of final assessment. The strategies needed for success were challenging for students who did not favour a left-brained thinking style but although this caused problems for right-brained thinkers such as dyslexic students, at least study skills tutors recognised the goal posts. However, assessment methods in higher education are fundamentally changing and this is no longer limited to individual subject requirements.

The most profound transformation to assessment methods is through the recent integration of digital communication. Communication technology for study programmes is widely available and is increasingly being used for teaching, learning and assessment. Students are being asked to interact with other students in online chatrooms, publish their coursework for peer assessment and produce blogs to demonstrate their learning. Study skills tuition is often unsuitable for such coursework, as it requires live communication on a regular basis, challenging dyslexic students who struggle with literacy skills and written expression. New approaches to assessment are also favoured due to the proliferation of websites selling written assignments, making academic dishonesty harder to identify. Higher education institutions are introducing innovative forms of assessment that are more reflective and personal in nature and therefore harder to falsify. Whilst institutions explore these new approaches, study skills tutors are faced with an influx of unfamiliar tasks to decipher that are outside their usual range of expertise.

## Emotional Distress Experienced by Dyslexic Students

The higher education sector has its own unique challenges for students with dyslexia. There are inevitable skills deficits that each dyslexic student has not yet overcome, combined with greater expectations for independent study and increased academic requirements. Many students with dyslexia have limiting beliefs about their abilities and these are amplified within the context of higher level study, causing significant anxiety and stress. Study skills tutors often report that the key to helping their students succeed is to help them build self-confidence, but when the barriers to learning are emotional, tutors themselves may feel out of their depth.

## Developing Coaching Skills

The use of coaching in education is relatively new and there are many different approaches currently in use. In the tradition of many new trends, sometimes the word 'teaching' is simply replaced with the word 'coaching', whilst providing no discernible difference in the application. In the same way that dyslexia tutors have developed specialist forms of teaching to enhance their students' learning, specialist coaching skills are also needed. A directive style of coaching, where advice is given and required behaviours are explained, will not address the challenges that exist in the higher education sector either for students or study skills tutors.

Sometimes tutors will not have the answers, but by developing a coaching style that provides expertise in asking powerful questions, they will have the skills needed to facilitate new discoveries. Such coaching skills enable complex tasks to be understood more clearly, broken down into their components and an action plan to be devised. In the current climate of constant change, study skills tutors need to be experts at helping students discover their inner resources and hidden capabilities in order to succeed with a diverse range of study demands.

For many adults with dyslexia, studying is not simply a cognitive process, it is an emotional trial that affects their self-esteem on many different levels. These challenges are intrinsically bound within their belief systems and are not easily solved with rational explanations or pep talks. A student who has experienced educational failure in the past may be unwilling to risk doing so again and may engage in patterns of avoidance and procrastination. Tutors need to be adept at building rapport, as dyslexic students may feel vulnerable about discussing their weaknesses. A coaching system is needed that engages with students' own internal processes, explores their deeper motivations and helps them mobilise their energy for study tasks. To make such changes possible, coaching must engage with underlying belief systems and provide the mechanisms for transforming them. It must also accept that overcoming emotional distress is an integral part of the learning process for some dyslexic students.

Most importantly, study skills tuition at higher education level needs to be valued as a complex and challenging role. It is not merely the process of imparting information; in order to be successful, tutors have to be adept at facilitating transformation. There is great potential for developing a coaching methodology that reflects these demands, as well as a timely recognition of the professional expertise required from individual tutors.

# Research

# New Insights into the Demography of Dyslexia – from Anecdote to Statistic

Al Campbell BSc., with statistical analysis by
Jonathan Plowden Roberts

Dyslexics like me, like numbers, unlike words, numbers always mean exactly the same thing. Once you get a grasp of that there is a lot of comfort in the simple language of arithmetic. As an aside algebra, with its eternal string of unknowns, can be much less friendly. Statistics, however, are wonderful things.

The problem with dyslexia is that it is very light on statistics. As a writer newly come to any subject it is always good to work with statistical fact – it means you can underpin opinion with unchanging numbers. Accordingly, when I first sat down to write a book on dyslexia I naturally had some big but basic questions in my mind:

- How many dyslexics are there?

- What proportion of the population is dyslexic?

- Are boys more dyslexic than girls?

Asking around and looking for references, both in person and on the web, the responses to these questions were mostly anecdotal. I related those anecdotes in my text and, by and large, nobody questioned them much as they seemed to be the perceived wisdom.

That perceived wisdom seemed to be:

- Somewhere between 1 in 8 and 1 in 10 people (so between 10% and 12.5% of the population is dyslexic) although recent research in the US has suggested it may be as many as 1 in 5 (Shaywitz 2003).

- Dyslexia is more common in boys than girls by a ratio of 3:1 – thus girls only account for 25% of dyslexics.

In follow-up one-to-one conversations about my book with practitioners I sensed, however, that these figures, especially the gender bias, gave cause for concern. My dyslexic sense of the inquisitive was once again stimulated and I decided to research the question further.

A major problem in working in a field like dyslexia is that people tend to work in small groups. As such, it is difficult to get big enough datasets for sample sizes to be statistically valid (typically you need a sample of 200 for results to be valid within two standard deviations). Moreover, in an area where there has been little formal recognition of the condition until recently, there are more significant problems. In the first place you can only work with the numbers of people who come forward for assessment (and who are prepared or resourced to pay for it) and this cohort may be just the tip of the iceberg. Secondly, some dyslexics present much more precociously than others. Finally, the focus tends to be on children – and quite understandably so. All these things potentially skew research.

However, some datasets are available, an analysis of which can at least put some statistical 'flags in the sand'. The following observations offer some headline insights from a larger piece of research that is still a work in progress in partnership with the Helen Arkell Dyslexia Centre, to be published in full at some future date. I do not propose to attempt to account in detail as to why the numbers that follow are what they are, although hopefully they will prompt debate. Rather, given the sample sizes in question, we can take them with confidence as snapshots of the certain aspects of the demography of dyslexia at the time period to which they refer.

## Analysis from the Helen Arkell Dyslexia Centre Database

Over the period 2002 to mid-2010 the Helen Arkell Dyslexia Centre (HADC) carried out over 6,000 dyslexia assessments, with total assessments carried out each year sufficient for statistical validity. These were across all age ranges, but predominantly from age 5–19 (banded ages 5–9, 10–14 and

15–19) quite evenly split at around +/- 30% cohorts. There was some minor variation from year to year.

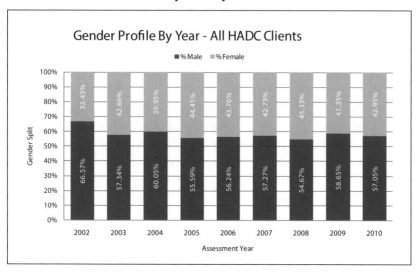

The chart clearly shows that contrary to the anecdotal gender split evidence there is only a small bias towards males being in the preponderance.

It was also possible to analyse the birth month of those assessed at HADC. There has always been strong anecdotal evidence that 'summer-born' children are more likely to be dyslexic and, whilst there seems to be no real difference in gender and birth month, it is clear from the 'total' line that from March through until August there is a definite spike in the likelihood of dyslexia.

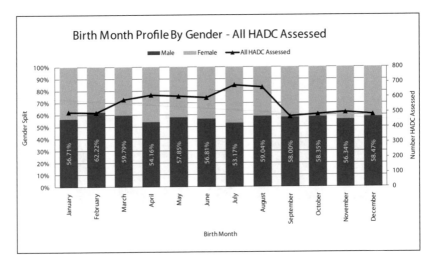

Birth Month Profile By Gender - All HADC Assessed

Other insights from the HADC database will be forthcoming.

## Analysis from the HESA Database

The Higher Education Statistics Agency (HESA) reports on the cohort of students in higher and further education. Among other data it has reported the number and gender of students who claim the Disabled Students Allowance (DSA) for reasons of a 'specific learning difficulty' (this was previously called 'dyslexia').

The sample size here is both substantial and significant, based on an undergraduate student population of around 750,000 and a dyslexic cohort approaching 25,000.

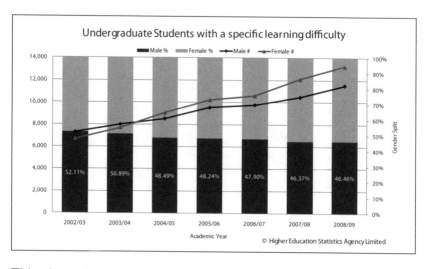

This chart clearly shows that by the time people enter university the cohort of female dyslexics not only exceeds the cohort of male dyslexics, but that it is increasing at a faster rate and that the differential is growing. Furthermore, at the time of going to press these numbers have not been calibrated against the total gender split in HE and FE – reports elsewhere suggest that females outnumber males, although the 'gender gap' may not be significant against the total sample size. In the years until 2009 the increase in dyslexics in HE was outstripping the growth in the student body as a whole.

## Caveats, Conundrums and Conclusions

At one level the HADC sample is skewed in several ways. Firstly, it only represents those who present for an assessment at HADC and are equipped to pay for it. HADC is in an affluent area of South East England and geographical factors should be taken into account. However, within the sample itself it is fair to assume a reasonably homogeneous population.

Perhaps the biggest conundrum is that of 'month of birth'. Scientifically it is hard to imagine a logical reason for this – it is akin to saying that dyslexia is related to your 'star sign'. If not 'nature' the only assumption that can be made is that it must be 'nurture' – in some way 'the system' is exposing those who are summer born.

With regard to the HESA statistics the numbers only cover those who have achieved the levels of academic success to proceed to tertiary education. There are two ways of looking at the numbers here. On the one hand, when dyslexics present for assessment they tend to demonstrate strong intellectual potential and would, therefore, seem more likely to achieve the grades required for university entry, especially with the allowances many now receive. On the other, specific learning difficulties are preventing dyslexics progressing.

Whatever the background, however, the total dyslexic population at university is still under 3.5%, or 1 in 28, although the trend shows it is growing steadily. In this case in order to get anywhere near the anecdotal figure of 1 in 10 throughout the total 18–23 cohort either the non-university population needs to be heavily dyslexic, or there need to be many 'anonymous' dyslexic students.

Other than the fact that statistics suggest the gender split in dyslexia is much closer to 50:50 there are few conclusions that can be drawn. Hopefully, however, the statistics presented here will make us better informed with regard to some of the questions.

### References

Shaywitz, S. (2003) *Overcoming Dyslexia*. New York, Vintage Books.

# Specific Learning Difficulties and Mental Health

Gilda Palti

The nature of the relationship between specific learning difficulties such as dyslexia and various social and mental health problems has been researched extensively during the last decade. A survey (Cummings et al. 1992) looking at various emotional difficulties such as depression, anxiety, low self-esteem and low self-concept revealed increased risk for mental health associated with specific learning difficulties in youths.

Demands to achieve academically put significant pressure on all students, but those with specific learning difficulties may be at particular risk of experiencing higher levels of stress. This may be due to several reasons, including the commonly noted remarks by significant others, such as parents and teachers, that the pupils do not put effort into school work, when in fact they try hard but cannot perform at their ability level. In addition, being tutored in a separate group with additional assistance and being dependent on others for academic success increases stress.

The gap between their ability and their performance in relation to others in class leads to the self-concept confusion. For example, they may perform well in class discussion but find it difficult to express their ideas in writing. This is accompanied by additional shame and embarrassment for writing less well than others in class. These difficulties cause enormous stress, as observed in a very bright 9-year-old boy who performed and worked well in various tasks which he found challenging and interesting, but when asked to produce a written task, the stress levels increased visibly and he asked to stop saying that: 'I am desperate to leave the room now', even when it was clear that the session had not ended.

As a result of school failure, parents, teachers and peers express disapproval or disappointment toward the pupils with specific learning difficulties, leading to feelings of inferiority, helplessness (Bruck 1986), lower self-concept and self-esteem (Kavale and Fomess 1996) and stress among these pupils.

Alexander-Passe (2007) in the School Situation Survey, investigated both the sources and manifestations of stress amongst dyslexic pupils and non-dyslexic sibling controls. Results suggest significant differences between the groups, with dyslexic pupils experiencing the highest stress levels, specifically in interactions with teachers, worries over academic examinations and performance testing, causing emotional (fear, shyness and loneliness) and physiological (nausea, tremors or rapid heartbeat) manifestations. (Alexander-Passe 2007).

Higher levels of anxiety, though not clinically significant, have also been found among pupils with specific learning difficulties (Fisher, Allen and Kose 1996). Anxiety leads to inability to relax, often having trouble falling or staying asleep. Worries may be accompanied by physical symptoms such as headaches, irritability, muscle tension, fatigue and problems with concentration.

Consistent and painful failures at school and developed feelings of helplessness, were found to be associated with depression among pupils with specific learning difficulties. Depressed pupils may exhibit irritability, poor concentration, sleep disturbance, intense feeling of sadness, lack of interest, fatigue, social withdrawal and suicidal thoughts. In a case of a 12-year-old boy recently diagnosed with dyslexia, the mother reported that she had caught him watching u-tube on how to commit suicide. The boy's comment was: 'I am not worth living because I am not good at anything', expressing a generalised feeling of worthlessness as a consequence of poor academic achievement. These feelings can create barriers to academic success consequently increasing the anxiety and lowering the self-concept, thus entering into a vicious circle which may with time magnify the symptoms. Anxiety and depression are highly related and high levels of anxiety have been shown to predispose depression (Hirschfeld et al. 1989; Kendler et al. 1993). However, it is important for professionals to be aware that the presentation of depression may be obscured by the symptoms of the specific learning difficulties, such as slow processing speed, memory and concentration problems.

Depression scales completed by parents and teachers were found to show a relatively higher depression mean score, though not clinically significant, for pupils with specific learning difficulties (McConaughy and Ritter 1985; McConaughy et al. 1994) compared with pupils not experiencing specific learning difficulties. Depression manifests differently in children than it does in adults. Symptoms of depression in children include hyperactivity, conduct problems, somatic complaints, or irritability, which make accurate diagnosis difficult (Colbert et al. 1982; Stevenson & Romney 1984).

There is a higher frequency rate for pupils with specific learning difficulties to be socially rejected than for those with no specific learning difficulties. Research indicates that social skills deficits are common in students with specific learning difficulties and that these deficits have a negative effect on these pupils' relationships with adults and peers, as well as on their ability to function in the regular classroom environment (Pearl et al. 1986).

## Attribution to Success and Failure

One reason for increased levels of emotional maladjustment is the attribution for success and failure made by pupils with specific learning difficulties. The importance of locus of control in education lies in the effect that it has on pupils' attitudes toward school-related tasks. Those with internal locus of control are found to exhibit high levels of perseverance on difficult tasks, to delay gratification and to seek and retain information (Dweck 1975). Conversely, children who possess an external locus of control generally feel that they have little impact on the outcome of tasks and that task difficulty, luck or fate control their success and failure. These pupils respond to difficult tasks with withdrawn behaviour, lowered task completion and negative self-concept (Dweck and Repucci 1973). Several studies have shown that individuals with specific learning difficulties attribute failure to internal factors, such as lack of ability and effort and success to external factors, such as luck (Kavale and Fomess 1996). This pattern of attribution leads to feelings of learned helplessness, placing these pupils at a higher level of risk for emotional maladjustment (Brooks 1994). Pupils that manage to deal effectively with stress demonstrate an internal locus of control (Luthar 1991), i.e. they believe in their ability to control the environment, rather than believing that the circumstances are determinative. Also, internal locus of control suggests that the individuals accept the responsibility for their own performance and as a result take an active part in dealing with stressful situations. They use their internal resources in the process of coping with stress.

Higher self-esteem and internal locus of control have been found to protect the student from both internalising and externalising problems. Their protective effect is more significant against depression when students experience academic failure (Roeser and Eccles 1997). The study provides evidence that self-esteem and locus of control are related to certain types of mental health that students tend to experience, such as those with higher self-esteem tend to have externalised problems (delinquent behaviour), than internalised problems (depression, anxiety).

Sometimes locus of control is seen as a stable, underlying personality construct, but this may be misleading, since the theory and research indicates that locus of control is largely learned. Some psychological and educational interventions have been found to produce shifts towards internal locus of control (e.g. outdoor education programs; Hans 2000; Hattie, Marsh, Neill & Richards 1997).

The more the pupils with learned helplessness put effort into problem solving without reaching any valid conclusion, the more the chances are that their cognitive system will opt to disengage from the uncomfortable situation and protect self-concept. Failing to solve the problem (which may raise negative emotions), compounded with the cognitive effort being used, deprives energy, or 'processing capacity' (Sigmund and Tobias 1965, in Covington 1992) from the cognitive resources focused at the problem, decreasing the probability that the problem will ever be solved. As a result, it is most probable that the individual will stop the process which he considers to be worthless and tiring and may become disengaged from the problem, thus reaching a state similar to cognitive demobilisation (Sedek and Kofta 1990) or cognitive exhaustion.

The suggestion here is that the learned helplessness is an informational processing phenomenon in which the individual is unable to reduce uncertainty; therefore, the cognitive resources are directed away from the task towards intruding thoughts and negative emotional arousal (such as anxiety) which may in turn interfere with future task performance.

## Intervention Programmes

Individuals with specific learning difficulties are at risk of failure not only academically but also socially and emotionally. Continuous experiences of academic failure lead to various emotional maladjustments such as anxiety, stress and depression. It was also found that (Palti 1998) being educationally better off for dyslexic pupils has an emotional and social cost. This may mean that their coping strategies with the prolonged stressful educational circumstances are ineffective or even generate new problems. Therefore, an intervention programme should consist not only of specific educational provision but also of specific emotional support or retraining of attributions to education. Having realistic expectations provides the pupils with a sense of control. The development of self-control goes hand-in-glove with self-esteem and success. Having realistic information provides a feeling that things can be done to help the situation.

Children are less defensive when the problem is cast as strategies that must be changed rather than as something deficient with their motivation. For example, a comment made by teachers or parents can be reframed, such that instead of saying: 'try harder and put in more of an effort' when many of them do try hard and still have difficulty, a comment like, 'we should find a better way to help you learn' may be more effective.

Individual therapy or counselling for attribution retraining could also be effective when introduced in conjunction with special educational provision. However, group therapy may sometimes be much more effective than individual therapy, because peers may be a better source of support and insight, especially peers with the same problem. Group and individual therapy may often be recommended to complement each other. When insight is gained in individual therapy, it can be exercised in the safe environment of a supportive small group. This is recommended because pupils with specific learning difficulties do not often have a chance to air the problems they experience without being judged or criticised, not only literacy problems, but also problems about making friends, feelings of isolation, shame or frustration. Because of the nature of their difficulties, many of these pupils have problems articulating their feelings and thoughts often get confused because they do not have the skills to verbalise them effectively. They may also have difficulties pointing to the source of their anger or frustration. Therefore, individual or group counselling or the combination of both may clear some of these uncertainties.

# Wobbles, Warbles and Fish – The Brain Basis of Dyslexia

John Stein

Some may think that this title is a trifle facetious, but its aim is to get you to think about the basic brain processing weaknesses that underlie reading difficulties: wobbles in visualising words, insensitivity to letter sound differences measured by listening to warbles and the overriding importance of good nutrition in the development of the brain, exemplified by eating fish. Many people still believe that problems learning to read are entirely due to phonological weaknesses, i.e. difficulty learning to translate letters into the sounds they stand for. Thus they believe that reading problems are primarily due to a high-level language problem, not dependent on basic visual and auditory sensory processing of the letters and their sounds. However, the very essence of reading is to translate letters into their sounds; so calling dyslexia a phonological problem merely restates the symptoms. What we really want to know is why so many children have these problems. That way we should be able to learn how to help them more.

Much of the processing required for reading is visual. Beginner readers need to learn to identify letters and their order in words and translate them into their sounds, in order to understand their meaning. This is the 'sublexical' or 'phonological' route. However, practised readers already have many words in their 'sight vocabularies', so that they can identify these words and their meaning entirely visually using the 'lexical' route, which is much faster. The important point here is that both routes draw heavily on visual processing. The lead component of visual processing in terms of timing is a system of large neurones called magnocells (m-) that rapidly direct your attention and your eyes to look at the letters and words being processed. There is now much evidence that development of this system is mildly impaired in many dyslexics; the cells do not end up in the right places in the brain and they work more slowly and inaccurately.

Since they are important for maintaining stable visual perception this means that children with visual magnocellular impairment find that letters appear to blur and move around, so they find them hard to identify, particularly their order.

Understanding the role of magnocells in these problems has helped us to develop effective ways of combating them. The simplest is to look through yellow or blue coloured filters. Although magnocells do not contribute to conscious colour vision, they receive their input mainly from the red and green cones in the retina, so that yellow filters that let through red and green light, but not blue, favour the magnocells. Some children immediately experience a dramatic improvement. 'The words were all blurry; now they're sharp and I can see them properly.' We find that about 25% of the children we see can be helped simply by using these Oxford yellow filters for all reading and close work. On average their reading increases by six months after three months wearing them. Often this has a permanent effect and they no longer need to use the filters thereafter.

Other children seem to benefit more from blue filters, however, probably by a different mechanism. Blue light selectively stimulates a recently discovered type of retinal ganglion cell, which contains the photopigment melanopsin. This means that they respond to blue light directly, although they also receive input from the retinal rods and cones. Their maximal sensitivity is at 450nm, which is precisely the peak transmission of our Oxford blue filters. Their function is to signal overall light levels to the body's internal clock situated in the suprachiasmatic nucleus (SCN) of the hypothalamus. This controls all our daily rhythms and its melanopsin cell input synchronises it to prevailing day length, arousing us earlier in summer and later in winter. This arousal is mediated by the SCN activating the magnocellular system. Hence blue filters worn for reading and close work in the morning and early afternoon can pep up the visual m- system and thus help to stabilise vision and make reading easier. We found that children who benefit from blue increased their reading age by nine months in three months.

Again the improvement was often permanent and they did not need to use the filters thereafter.

In accordance with our hypothesis we also found that these children's sleep patterns improved greatly and with it their tiredness during the day decreased. More unexpectedly we found that the children ceased getting so many headaches. In some cases the mothers who suffered from migraine also tried the blue glasses and found that their headaches improved as well. Recently it has been shown that migrainous headaches are often associated with disturbed sleep patterns and abnormal operation of the SCN clock. So this provided more evidence that our blue glasses work by improving SCN synchronisation to prevailing day length.

However, only about half of the children we see benefit from coloured filters. The majority of the others do not complain of any visual symptoms at all. In contrast, they often give a history of mispronunciation and mis-sequencing of word sounds, sometimes bringing them to the attention of speech therapists. Identifying phonemes and their order depends on the auditory equivalent of visual magnocells in the brain. These large cells in the auditory system can track the rapid changes in sound frequency and amplitude that convey the different letter sounds. These auditory magnocells derive from the same developmental lineage as the visual ones and their development seems to be impaired in many dyslexics. Armed with this knowledge we can understand why dyslexics' auditory sensitivity can often be improved by seemingly bizarre treatments, such as listening to classical music and learning to drum rhythmically; these all help to improve the segmentation, identification and sequencing of sounds.

In order to understand dyslexia better, we are also interested in why these magnocellular cells fail to develop normally. The most powerful single influence is genetic; dyslexia runs strongly in families and twin studies have shown that 50% of people's differences in reading ability are inherited. In Oxford we have the technology to analyse which genes are associated with reading problems and we have identified two new gene variants associated with hereditary poor reading. One, known as KIAA 0319 situated on the short arm of chromosome 6, we've shown to be important in guiding the distribution of nerve cells in the brain during early development. This, together with other genes shown to be associated with dyslexia, such as DCD2 also on chromosome 6 and ROBO, explains why the m- cells often end up in the wrong places in dyslexia.

The other new gene that we've found on chromosome 18 seems to interact with the most important environmental influence of all, namely nutrition. M-cells are particularly vulnerable to lack of the membrane omega 3 fatty acids, EPA & DHA that usually come from eating oily fish. But very few people eat much fish nowadays. We've found that giving these omega 3 fish oil supplements to poor readers can often dramatically help them to focus their attention more accurately and thus overcome their reading difficulties.

# International Perspectives

# Dyslexia: International Perspectives: From Pain to Power

Gavin Reid

## Background

There has been significant progress over the last twenty years in the development of policy and provision for dyslexia. Previously, dyslexia was seen as a 'cause' – promoted by desperate parents, lobbying for recognition of dyslexia so that those in power could acknowledge the educational and emotional needs of children with dyslexia. Identification and particularly early identification, became a major issue, just in fact as it is now!

Parents' groups have become a powerful player in the development of policy and practice in the UK and elsewhere. The progress in the UK has been exceptional and the good practice which is becoming more widespread is a model for other countries in Europe and Asia. The BDA system of teacher training accreditation and the quality kite marks of AMBDA and the 'dyslexia-friendly' schools campaign have ensured that dyslexia is at the forefront of agendas influencing educational policy and practice in the UK. I recall an article I wrote for the Times Educational Supplement in 1988 headed 'Dyslexia: A Suitable Case for Training' – it was met with some derisory comment by colleagues at the time and although courses had been held by the independent voluntary organisations these had yet to penetrate the state school system. How different the situation is now – at least in the UK – where government is actually requesting that such courses (Rose Report on dyslexia 2009) be run and providing funding to ensure implementation and in Scotland the Scottish Executive produced a report on dyslexia identifying areas for development, including training (Scottish Executive 2009).

But it is important not to be complacent about such progress. There are still areas of discontent and helplines run by the BDA, Dyslexia Scotland and branches of the BDA throughout the country are still overrun with calls from desperate parents. But the situation in the UK is still rosy in comparison with some other countries. The Czech Republic, for example, in their definition of learning disabilities clusters a range of conditions including Developmental Learning Disabilities into a chronic health category (Minister for Health and Sport 2008/9). This in fact is a trend among a number of European countries, although the extended membership of the European Union has resulted in a number of innovative collaborative EU projects including those with new member states. An example of this is the 'Training Programme for Parents, Teachers and Psychologists working with Children affected by Dyslexia' project and is prepared as a Grundtvig Learning Partnership project under the EU 'Lifelong Learning Programme'. The aim of the project is to produce a training guide for teachers/trainers/psychologists and parents of pupils (6–10 years old) affected by dyslexia that corresponds with EU standards in collaboration with international partners and institutions (**http://dyslexia.europole.org/**). The DYPATEC Grundvig project has also produced a parents' guide on dyslexia following a European-funded, collaborative project designed to develop educational, social and cultural integration (**http://www.dyspel.org/dypatec/index.php?de**). The independent and voluntary organisations have had a significant influence in the development of projects, materials and dissemination of materials through conferences and sponsored events. For example, Dyslexia International (formerly DITT) and the Dyslexia Foundation of New Zealand have both had an influence on recognition of dyslexia and on policy in different parts of the world and there are many other examples of this in different countries.

## Initiatives

A high note was struck in New Zealand when the government officially recognised dyslexia in 2007. Much of this success is due to the pressure and the hard work of the Dyslexia Foundation of New Zealand (DFNZ) (**http://www.dyslexiafoundation.org.nz/**) who are utilising a three-pronged policy of recognition, understanding and action as well as the long-standing efforts of SPELD in New Zealand. Since its acceptance of the term 'dyslexia' in 2007, the NZ Ministry of Education (MOE) has taken steps to support students with the label in the school system. The MOE completed a literature review in 2007 and came to the conclusion that dyslexia, although having a range of presenting needs, shows in children as a phonological deficit. Since 2007 the Dyslexia Foundation of New Zealand (DFNZ) has lobbied for change and support within the school system for students that have dyslexia.

An innovative scheme was initiated by the Nova Scotia Department of Education in Canada when they developed a strategy aimed at co-ordination of resources and identifying and disseminating best practice in Learning Disabilities (LD). They appointed an LD consultant to work within the Provincial LD strategy. The consultant had an important role and is responsible for the evaluation of the effectiveness of practice, such as the additional tuition support programmes that are being offered and for developing, co-ordinating and monitoring new initiatives.

In Singapore the Dyslexia Association of Singapore has aspired to run a systematic service of identification, intervention and training and seminars. This all-embracing service has been the result of many years of hard work by the team in Singapore. Similarly, the Hong Kong Dyslexia Association have continued with a series of workshops for parents and teachers and have been very much involved in promoting the needs of children with dyslexia in that area.

## Identification and Intervention

The issues regarding identification of dyslexia are universal. One of the main points that have motivated governments to action has been the long-standing reliance on the 'wait-to-fail' model (Crombie and Reid 2009). This has resulted in children waiting months and years to be formally diagnosed. This highlights the need for dyslexia awareness and early identification and in fact underpins the BDA 'dyslexia-friendly' campaign as 'informed' teachers who can facilitate earlier awareness and recognition of dyslexia.

This has been the rationale for many of the initiatives throughout the world. In the Middle East innovative approaches have been noted in Kuwait in particular. The Center for Child Evaluation and Teaching (CCET) in Kuwait **(http://www.ccetkuwait. org)** is rapidly becoming a world leader in the development of assessment materials, publications, training and research. Initiatives such as those are much needed in the Middle East and the work of the CCET holds great promise for the future. One of the key aims of the CCET is to develop fine-tuned assessment materials to identify children with dyslexia, but also to develop early screening materials and teacher awareness of dyslexia to prevent failure from occurring. This is one of the reasons for the development of the PG diploma training course developed by the CCET. Screening work in Arabic has also been carried out by the Kuwait Dyslexia Association. This theme of promoting early identification and teacher awareness has been highlighted in a number of countries.

The Learning Disabilities Association of Canada (LDAC) completed a study in 2007 looking at Canadians with learning disabilities (LD) and how the LD affects their lives. One key observation made was that the 'wait-to-fail' model was not working and there needed to be 'early screening and early intervention for all Canadian schoolchildren' (Learning Disabilities Association of Canada 2007, para. 8).

The ambitious project in Scotland spearheaded by Dyslexia Scotland on assessment has attempted to provide a teacher-led assessment protocol combined with top quality training. The scheme launched in June 2010 will need time to take a firm hold, but it offers great promise.

The Response to Intervention (RTI) model used in the United States offers early intervention to all students based on an 'at risk' model. Once identified, these students are given the support, but the RTI model necessitates trained teachers to run it efficiently and effectively. This in itself takes funding and a long-term commitment from both the school district and the government and the research on this is currently quite mixed and there are a number of issues still to be resolved (Thomson 2010).

In terms of intervention the momentum from the National Reading Panel in the USA (NICHD 2000) has had an impact throughout the decade. The panel indicated that effective reading instruction includes: teaching children to manipulate the sounds in words (phonemic awareness), teaching them that these sounds are represented by letters of the alphabet which can then be blended together to form words (phonics) and applying strategies to guide and improve reading comprehension. This position has been promoted by The International Dyslexia Association (IDA) and the national organisations of Orton Gillingham (OG) tutors in the USA and in Canada and is not unlike the impetus gained in some areas from the UK, Rose Report.

## Conclusion

The World Dyslexia Forum, 3–5 February 2010, at UNESCO, Paris was a major international initiative that took place in 2010 (**http://www.worlddyslexiaforum.org/**). The forum advocated for teachers to be better trained and equipped to allow them to tackle the needs of children and adults with dyslexia as well as other learning difficulties. They noted in their summary of the conference that it had been reported that 'some countries have begun to recognise the problem but, in general, provision remains uneven'. Yet international collaboration is widespread, good practice has and continues to be, disseminated and areas which have been sadly neglected such as multilingualism have been prioritised – so although recognition and provision may be 'uneven' the outlook for the future holds great promise that the needs of children and adults with dyslexia will be understood.

## References

Crombie, M. and Reid, G. (2009) The Role of Early Identification: Models for Research and Practice. In G. Reid, G. Elbeheri, J. Everatt, J. Wearmouth, D. Knight (eds.) *The Routledge Companion to Dyslexia*. London, Routledge.

NICHD (2000)

Report of the National Reading Panel. Teaching Children to
    Read: An evidence-based assessment of the scientific
    research literature on reading and its Implications for reading
    instruction: Reports of the sub-groups. Washington D.C. U.S.
    Government Printing Office.

Reid, G. (1988) Dyslexia: A Case for Training. Times Educational
    Supplement 26th February.

Rose, J. (2009) Identifying and Teaching Children and Young
    People with Dyslexia and Literacy Difficulties. London,
    Department for Children, Schools and Families.

Scottish Executive (2009) Education for Learners with Dyslexia.
    K, HMIE. http://www.hmie.gov.uk/documents/publication/
    eflwd.html

Thomson, J. (2010) Good Practice in Interventions for Teaching
    Dyslexic Learners and in Teacher Training in English-
    speaking paper presented at the World Dyslexia Forum,
    3–5 February 2010 http://www.worlddyslexiaforum.org/

Dr. Gavin Reid is an independent educational psychologist,
    international seminar presenter and author. His website is
    www.drgavinreid.com

# Recognition and Support for Children with Special Educational Needs in Cyprus

Pantelitsa Paphiti

## Introduction

Although there are a number of definitions attempting to describe dyslexia, for the purposes of the current article *dyslexia* would be considered as:

'A processing difference experienced by people of all ages, often characterised by difficulties in literacy, it can affect other cognitive areas such as memory, speed of processing, time management, co-ordination and directional aspects. There may be visual and phonological difficulties and there is usually some discrepancy in performances in different areas of learning. It is important that the individual differences and learning styles are acknowledged since these will affect outcomes of assessment and learning. It is also important to consider the learning and work context as the nature of the difficulties associated with dyslexia may be more pronounced in some learning situations' (Reid 2003: p.5).

In this definition, dyslexia is reconceptualised in terms of preventative and descriptive criteria and gives a multi-disciplinary framework for intervention (Crombie (2002) cited by Reid (2003)), taking into consideration learning styles and environmental factors. Practitioners can benefit from this definition since it gives a plethora of behavioural indicators, pointing towards an early identification.

### Special Education Policy in Cyprus

In Cyprus the state is responsible for providing free compulsory education to children from the age of 4 years 8 months up to the age of 15. It offers education in nursery, primary, secondary and post 16. All levels of education are under the authority of the Ministry of Education and Culture, which is responsible for educational policy making.

The policy for Special Education in Cyprus is expressed within the Special Education Law 113(I) of 1999, the Regulations for the Early Detection of Children with Special Needs 185(1)/2001 and the Regulations for the Training and Education of Children with Special Needs 186(1)/2001. These last two regulate the implementation of the new law as from September 2001.

Through the core articles of the Law for Special Education, the state recognises that all children have a right to an education appropriate to their needs. The state attempts to provide a legal framework where those with special educational requirements can receive, in the least restrictive environment, an education which meets their individual needs.

According to Law 13(1)/1999, a child with special needs means a child who exhibits serious or special learning, functional or adaptive difficulty, due to bodily (sensory nerves included), mental or psychical deficiencies and who requires the provision of special education and training.

## Procedure

'A child is considered to have special educational needs if he/she has a significantly greater difficulty in learning than the majority of children of a similar age or if a disability prevents or impedes him/her from using the standard educational facilities and resources available in mainstream schools' (Law 113 of 1999).

In this case, the child is referred to a District Committee for special Education and Training which will assess the child and evaluate its needs. The Committee will conduct a full multi-disciplinary team assessment and will also operate to provide all the necessary measures in terms of curriculum adaptation, technical and staffing support for the effective education of the children within a mainstream setting.

The multidisciplinary team conducting the assessment consists of a child psychologist, an educational psychologist, a teacher of special education, a doctor, a speech therapist and any other specialist, as the case may need. The District Committee decides whether a child is in need of special education and training or additional facilities. It also decides whether special education and training shall be provided in mainstream classroom, in a special unit in mainstream schools or in a special school.

Special education and training means provision of the necessary assistance to a child with special needs aiming at his complete development in all fields, particularly the psychological, social and learning and at the provision of pre-professional and professional training in schools, where this is possible.

Special education and training includes among others, teaching of everyday skills of self-care, personal hygiene, transportation, linguistic development and communication, emotional improvement and generally provision of all means, equipment and human resources, aiming towards a child's school and social integration and independent life.

According to the Law for Special Education and Training of 1999, children, to whom special education and training has been determined, attend ordinary schools, special units (classes in mainstream schools, usually with children who have similar problems such as autism) or special schools with appropriate infrastructure, adapted to their own needs. In Cyprus there are only nine special schools, since the educational policy of the Ministry of Education and Culture with regard to children with special needs, is their integration in schools of general education.

Children with specific learning difficulties – dyslexia – attend mainstream schools and follow the normal curriculum, which may be adjusted to suit their particular needs, according to the child's Individual Education Plan (IEP). The IEP gives a detailed analysis of general goals for each subject. Each goal is subdivided into specific targets and ways of achieving them. The teacher must report on the IEP giving dates of assessment and at the end of each semester must evaluate the targets regarding the child's progress. At the end of the year the teacher must give a final report, as part of the IEP, regarding the overall progress and the child's status.

Access to the curriculum is personalised according to individual needs. Where a child requires individual assistance outside of his/her classroom, this is arranged so as not to restrict their access to all subjects of the curriculum.

## Teaching Framework

The individual assistance outside the classroom in primary schools is given by special educators. Teachers of special education who can be employed to provide services to children with specific learning difficulties/dyslexia, within mainstream primary schools, special units attached to mainstream schools or in special schools are classified as specialising in teaching children with specific learning, functional, adjusting difficulties. They can either have a bachelor's degree in education and a master's degree in special education or a bachelor's degree in special education.

Further special education teachers, depending on their educational background, are classified in the following areas of expertise: teaching children with visual impairments, teaching children with hearing impairment, speech therapy, special physical education, psychology, physiotherapy, music therapy, occupational therapy and audiology.

In secondary education, subject teachers provide support for children with special needs. A programme of seminars regarding special education is being developed to assist them in this task.

## Cyprus Association for Dyslexia

The Cyprus Association for Dyslexia, a non-profit organisation which was founded in 1993, embraces people with learning difficulties and particularly those with dyslexia. The main objectives of the Cyprus Association for Dyslexia are to help people who have characteristics of dyslexia to develop educational, intellectual and other capabilities. They mobilise the authorities to formulate and implement sound public policy on the issue of specific learning difficulties, to enlighten and educate the public and to facilitate the creation of a Diagnostic, Research and Rehabilitation Center for Dyslexia.

## Ending

Concluding, one can clearly state that the goal of all the efforts made here in Cyprus for early identification and support of children with specific educational needs, is to create the right conditions where these children can develop their skills and experience a happy present and a promising future.

## Bibliography

Reid, G. (2003) *Dyslexia: A Practitioner's Handbook*, (3rd edn). Chichester, John Wiley and Sons.

*The Education and Training of Children with Special Needs Law of 1999*

http://www.moec.gov.cy/eidiki/nomothesia/
Number_113(I)_1999.pdf

# Technology

# Technology Providing Access for All

Nasser Siabi

Technology is now an embedded part of every young person's learning. Computers and the internet enable learners to gain the skills they will need to become effective participants in an increasingly global economy that's pretty much becoming reliant on individuals' digital capabilities.

Despite the visual appeal and inclusive options that a multimedia approach to presenting information offers, most websites, text books and printed material still rely heavily on text to convey their messages.

There are a large number of learners who have problems when it comes to reading and writing and a group of learners whose needs are so specific that they cannot gain the full benefit of access to these fantastic resources or even essential course material.

Fortunately, technology can provide an opportunity for all learners to fully participate in learning and for those who need specialist support, it can also make the difference between being able to participate or not!

The good news is that with all modern computers, this is easy and inexpensive to do for the majority of learners who have reading and writing difficulties. Also, an added bonus is that by providing support for this group, it also offers opportunities for others to gain even more benefit from using the internet or other printed material.

## Accessibility 'Out of the Box'

Take a look at the accessibility features offered in a standard 'out of the box' Windows or Mac computer. Both types of machine offer many levels of customisation for users who have difficulty with reading and writing. The Ease of Access Centre within Windows 7 allows quick access to adjust accessibility settings on the computer for individuals. Apple also offers a variety of built-in tools and technologies that help all people to get the most from their computer.

Features that are offered with both of these operating systems include:

- Screen magnification which enlarges text size for those with low vision.

- Settings to increase and decrease contrast, remove colour (switch to greyscale) and even reverse the video to white-on-black or black-on-white for low vision users.

- On-screen keyboards, assignable mouse buttons and sticky keys which allow greater flexibility for those who have difficulty with physical access, or those who cannot easily avert their eyes from the screen without losing concentration.

- Text-to-speech options allow the computer to read back sections of the screen and to speak selected text on websites and within word processors with a single keystroke.

- Speech to text software allows voice control of the computer and also allows the user to speak directly into a word processor. This is useful for anyone who finds it difficult to use a keyboard and mouse, but also great for reluctant writers.

- Word completion and spell checking options within the accessibility options allow for improved efficiency with writing and recording.

- It is even possible to convert text to a spoken track that can be used on an MP3 player or Smartphone without having to purchase any additional software. Suddenly text becomes accessible for a range of users who prefer to have text read back to them, not just those who have difficulty with reading.

If you don't know what options and preferences are available, then there are also several presets already for you to choose from. It is then possible to further customise the preset so that it is exactly what you want. Once the computer has been setup as you like it, then your personal profile can be saved and stored so that it is available each time you log onto that machine. And if you are working on a network in a school, for example, it is also possible to have a 'roaming' profile that follows you wherever you log onto a computer on that network.

Many of these access features are also being built into portable devices such as Smartphones and MP3 players. Also there are many 'apps' available for these devices which help to improve accessibility of text. (Perhaps the focus of another article!)

## Other Basic Tools

Despite the improved accessibility built into modern computer operating systems, there are some additional software tools that all learners should have access to if they are going to take full advantage of the powerful role that technology can play in supporting reading and writing.

There are many software packages available for dyslexics and each has its own unique selling point or offers specific features that may help to overcome a particular reading or writing difficulty. The catalogue produced by the B.D.A. New Technologies Committee is a valuable resource for a product overview. However, there are a number of key areas that should be covered when deciding what other software tools should be installed on a computer to ensure that it is 'reading and writing friendly'.

Some of these features may be part of the computer operating system, but may be more suited to the learners needs when integrated into other software packages as often they include additional features. However, as a minimum, it is important to ensure that the areas below are covered:

- **Text to speech** software: for users who prefer to have pages of text read out loud. This could be web pages, worksheets or text books. It is also worthwhile checking to see if the software can read out pdf's. This file type is increasingly being used on the web to ensure that the layout of the document is maintained, particularly when it is a downloadable file. (Some text to speech software will not read pdf's).

- **Text prediction** software: (similar to 'predictive texting' on a phone) which helps to speed up writing. This is particularly useful for younger or reluctant writers. Many word processors now offer text prediction and word completion, but there are also software packages available that offer more than simple word prediction and will help with homophone checking, grammar checking and allow the user to create personal word banks.

- **Mind mapping** software: helps learners to structure, visualise and classify ideas and can be used as an aid to study, problem solving, decision-making and writing. Learners can then use the maps as revision aids, story boards for structuring essays and project planning.

- **Screen magnification** software: which enlarges any chosen section of the computer screen for learners who have sight impairments. Also great for reading in groups around one screen, or for 'family time' around the computer.

## So Much More than Technology for Dyslexics

When it comes to using technology to provide access to reading and writing it is important to think about supporting the needs of everyone who may use that particular computer. By providing a basic set of tools as outlined above and by customising the operating system for individual needs, you will be providing access to a much wider group of learners, while also providing specific support for those who need it.

# The Dyslexia Revolution: A New Era in Text Correction

Sharon Givon

There is a quiet revolution underway in the world of learning difficulties – but this revolution is not a new teaching technique or coping mechanism. Instead and perhaps surprisingly, it is a software company that is providing new hope to people with dyslexia.

According to the British Dyslexia Association, 10% of Britons suffer from dyslexia and 4% severely so. Thus dyslexia is a real disability, affecting the lives of millions, but its effects are often hidden. Those without learning difficulties themselves can fail to understand the nature of the condition and as a result do not realise the role dyslexia plays in the performance of certain tasks. It can thus blight people's lives and dyslexics may have to make substantial efforts to overcome the barriers which are (often unintentionally) put in their way.

The advent of computer spell checkers proved to be a very useful tool for writers, enabling them to produce texts with lower error rates. This, however, is not the case for people who suffer from dyslexia as traditional spell checkers are unable to recognise their misspellings, making incorrect or misleading suggestions. Moreover, it has been shown that up to 63% of the errors made by people with learning difficulties may not be detected at all by spell checkers (MacArthur et al. 1996).

Current technological solutions include text-to-speech (TTS) and speech-to-text (STT) software. Both of these approaches, however, have significant limitations. The accuracy of state-of-the-art STT systems is still facing major challenges. Moreover, recognition accuracy has reached its current plateau of 80% in 2001 and no significant improvement has been reported since[1]. TTS techniques cannot identify the majority of misused words

---

1 http://www.itl.nist.gov/iad/mig/publications/ASRhistory/index.html

and spelling mistakes. Therefore, the two methods can only offer little help to writers.

## Ineffective Technology: The Problem of Context and Dimensionality

The history of automatic spell checking and text correction is a mixed one. Traditional spell checkers work by comparing words, one word at a time, with a dictionary. If the word is not found, it is flagged as an error and a simple algorithm (such as Levenshtein distance) is used to generate a recommendation.

This technology has worked well for non-dyslexic users, with English as their first language. Casual errors are easily detected and quickly corrected. It poses certain unique difficulties for dyslexic users, though. Consider the following sentences:

'This will effect their score'
'This will affect their score'

The first sentence incorrectly uses the noun 'effects', in place of the verb 'affect'. A traditional spell checker is powerless here – both sentences are grammatically correct, but the first sentence has no meaning. Only knowledge of context can spot the mistake.

Consider the next example:

'My father teaches fizix'
'My father teaches physics'

The first sentence contains the phonetic spelling error 'fizix'. Traditional methods rely solely on letter similarity measures, but 'fizix' and 'physics' share only one letter – 'i'. In other words, the error and the correction are too different and, therefore, a traditional tool cannot identify the right word. A contextual spell checker on the other hand takes into consideration the neighbouring words and other linguistic features. Such spell checkers can successfully identify that the correction here is 'physics'.

A further problem arises when too many words are included in the dictionary – as more unusual words are included, the chances of a misspelt word being recognised as a correct but different word increases. This is the problem of dimensionality.

## A New Start

To solve this problem, it is necessary to define what an 'ideal world' text correction tool would be able to do:

1) Detect errors in spelling, even if the misspelled word actually exists in the dictionary.

2) Detect errors in phonetic spelling.

3) Detect errors in grammar.

4) Detect errors arising from the misuse of words.

5) Provide suggestions that make sense in the given context.

Let us examine these in further detail. Consider the following sentence (errors highlighted in red):

'Eddie licks to drinks only minerals water'

Microsoft Word for instance, at the time of writing, was completely unable to correct this sentence, not least because it cannot find any errors in it. Traditionally it would require a (non-dyslexic) human editor to spot errors of this nature – or a very substantial effort on behalf of a dyslexic user. This is because all the words exist in the dictionary and furthermore, the sentence is grammatical. The fact that it is nonsense to say 'Eddie licks to drinks' or 'Only minerals water' is not spotted, because Word does not understand the context.

Even in instances where a traditional spell checker detects an error, it does not necessarily have the capability to fix it. Consider the following:

'Im not shoor we can do eat.'

Word spots two of the three errors in this sentence, but if you accept the default corrections, you would get the following:

'I'm not shoo we can do eat.'

This is clearly not particularly helpful. What's more, if you look at the entire list of possible corrections that Word provides for 'shoor', the correct word, 'sure', does not even appear on the list! Fortunately for dyslexic people, Ginger Software has a tool that can correct these errors (and corrects all the examples above without mistakes).

## Ginger Software – A New Way

Ginger Software is a software company that is at the heart of a quietly growing revolution in the world of assistive technology. They provide a contextual grammar and spell checker which uses advanced artificial intelligence techniques to correct entire sentences based on context. If this sounds technical in concept, in practice it could not be simpler. You just type in text with errors and it corrects it at an unprecedented level of accuracy.

Ginger does this by looking at the whole sentence and working out from context which words are incorrect. It then automatically corrects unusual spelling mistakes, misused words and grammar errors.

This may sound like magic, but it seems even more amazing when you see it in action. It seems to effortlessly identify mistakes that most programs miss, or incorrectly identify and its use can be a transformative revelation for people with dyslexia. Yael Karov, the CEO and founder of Ginger Software, said: 'Ginger provides a life-changing experience for children and adults with learning difficulties. With Ginger, many people are able, perhaps for the first time in their lives, to independently produce error-free text'.

Indeed, a commercial version of Ginger Software has been available for a little over a year and already messages of support and thanks are pouring in. Hundreds of thousands of people all around the world are already enjoying the software and the company's customer base is growing rapidly. Karin, an undergraduate student at Brunel University in London, purchased Ginger Software through the Disabled Students Allowance scheme. 'I am dyslexic and have difficulty structuring sentences and I have also faced grammatical problems which have left me behind in my coursework', she told us. 'I now use Ginger Software, which helps me tremendously and gives me feedback about my mistakes. I think Ginger Software is brilliant for dyslexic people.'

Look at the following set of examples and ask yourself, could your spell checker correct these errors?

1) 'The djadje ruled agenst him.' MS Word corrects this to 'The jade ruled agents him.', whereas Ginger automatically considers the context and corrects the sentence to 'The judge ruled against him.'

2) 'Wer are you. You wer there. I wer my uniform.' MS Word again mistakenly corrects this to 'War are you. You war there. I war my uniform.' Because Ginger understands context, it is able to get the correct word in each sentence: 'Where are you. You were there. I wear my uniform.'

Ginger is designed as a writing and learning platform. In addition to correcting the errors that users make Ginger also provides reports of the users' frequent errors over time. The reports contain statistical error analyses based on the users' work experience. The software also features a TTS component which allows users to listen to individual words, sentences or full texts. Ginger software works in MS Word, Outlook, PowerPoint, IE as well as Firefox.

It is worth noting that Ginger does not yield perfect accuracy. Any program, no matter how advanced, will always make mistakes while it lacks a human-level understanding of text. But it is unquestionably a new dawn in text correction.

To learn more about Ginger Software, please visit their website: **www.gingersoftware.com**

## References

MacArthur, C. A., Graham, S., Haynes, J. B. & DeLaPaz, S. (1996). Spell Checkers and Students with Learning Disabilities: Performance Comparisons and Impact on Spelling. Journal of Special Education, 30, pp35 – 57.

## About the Author

Sharon has over a decade of experience in the domain of Natural Language Processing (NLP)-based products. She has an MSc in Speech and Language Processing and is currently writing up her doctorate thesis in the field of Computational Linguistics at the School of Informatics at Edinburgh University, Scotland.

**Bredon School**

Pull Court, Bushley, Tewkesbury, Gloucestershire. GL20 6AH

Telephone: +44 (0) 1684 293156 Fax: +44 (0)1684 276392
Email: enquiries@bredonschool.co.uk www.bredonschool.org

Bredon School is a mainstream co-educational day and boarding school for pupils between the ages of 4 and 18. Bredon has always welcomed children who have struggled at their previous schools, helping them to thrive by focusing on their individual talents and abilities. It has also gained an international reputation for its work with children with dyslexia and other Specific Learning Difficulties, such as dyspraxia.

- Small class sizes with a teacher:pupil ratio of 1:7
- Specialist experience and resources to support pupils with dyslexia
- Wide choice of academic and vocational courses available
- Full working farm and 13 acre forest school
- Wide range of sports and extra-curricular activities offered
- Set in 84 acres of landscaped grounds surrounding picturesque Pull Court

# Organisations

# Dyslexia Scotland

Cathy Magee

Dyslexia Scotland aims to encourage and enable children, young people and adults with dyslexia to reach their potential in education, employment and life. Based in Stirling, our network of volunteer-led local branches (currently 12 and growing) across Scotland offers support at a grassroots level.

Our three key aims are set out in our current Strategic Plan:

1) **Offering high quality services** at national and local levels.

2) **Influencing national positive change.**

3) **Supporting and sustaining** our network of branches, members and volunteers.

Key highlights of 2009/10 include:

- A newly designed, more accessible website.

- A comprehensive online 'Assessing Dyslexia' toolkit launched by Sir Jackie Stewart and Mike Russell, Cabinet Secretary for Education and Lifelong Learning in June 2010. It will help all teachers to identify literacy difficulties early. **http://www.frameworkforinclusion.org/AssessingDyslexia/**

- Performances by a dyslexic rapper of his dyslexia CD, *'Can't Hold Me Down'* in 40 schools and colleges across Scotland.

- A pilot project spearheaded by Sir Jackie Stewart to encourage prisoners at an Edinburgh prison to take up learning opportunities.

- An innovative podcast revision project enabling students at Lochaber High school to access revision notes in audio format. **http://lhs.typepad.co.uk/weblog/**

For further details contact:

Dyslexia Scotland, Stirling Business Centre, Wellgreen, Stirling, FK8 2DZ.

Email: **info@dyslexiascotland.org.uk**

Website: **www.dyslexiascotland.org.uk**

Telephone: 01786 44 66 50

Dyslexia Scotland Helpline: 0844 800 84 84

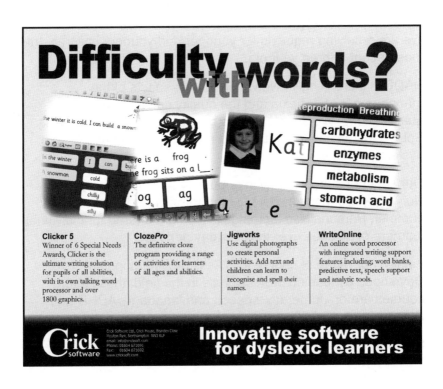

# Helen Arkell Dyslexia Centre

Bernadette McLean

2010 and 2011 see celebrations of Helen Arkell's 90th birthday and the Centre's 40th anniversary.

HADC's suite of professional course continues to grow, benefiting from the government funding for specialist teachers.

In addition to Specialist Teacher Training, the Centre continues to offer subsidised consultations, assessments by a range of trained professionals and specialist tuition.

Consultations are offered to parents, concerned about their children and to adults worried about their studies or their employment.

Our team of assessors has expanded further and we have developed an effective mentoring system for new assessors. We are receiving requests for younger and younger children, the most recent a three year old.

HADC is increasingly involved in many aspects of the management of dyslexia and the quality control of relevant qualifications. We are pleased to be a member of the Dyslexia SpLD Trust, a consortium of lead players in the world of dyslexia.

Our summer schools grow in popularity and we maintain our Norwegian connections by taking our training to Norway last summer. Personalised learning classes are offered for individual learners of all ages over their holiday periods.

Finally, our range of course for TAs is proving popular. Developed by leading professionals in the field, these short courses are on numeracy, speech and language, ADHD and Dyspraxia.

For further details see: **www.helenarkelldyslexiacentre.org**

# Patoss – Specialist Teachers Supporting Children and Young People with Dyslexia

Lynn Greenwold

As the Professional Association of Teachers of Students with Specific Learning Difficulties, Patoss is for all those concerned with the teaching and support of pupils with SpLD: dyslexia, dyspraxia, attention deficit disorder and Asperger's syndrome. We aim to promote good practice amongst professionals and have published guidelines for those moving into this field as well as for parents and established practitioners.

## The Challenge to Meet – a Specialist Teacher in Every School

A key goal of the Rose review is 'to provide substantially improved access to specialist expertise in all schools and across all local authority areas' (DCSF 2009: p.19). Patoss' full and associate members have gained qualifications which meet these standards for specialist teachers. Their specialist work includes evaluating students' current skills, planning and delivering teaching, advising on broader educational needs and, significantly, working with other professionals in schools to support mainstream literacy teaching. Membership supports teachers to keep up to date with developments in the field and is one way employers can be assured their teachers are appropriately qualified staff.

## The SpLD Assessment Practising Certificate

It is also crucial that all schools have easy and regular access to a specialist who is qualified to provide diagnostic assessment of students, to establish the nature of a literacy difficulty, carry out specialist teaching and recommend other support needs. In addition, all students with dyslexia wishing to apply for support at university through Disabled Students' Allowances will require a diagnostic assessment conducted since they were age 16. Those who hold a current SpLD Assessment Practising Certificate are suitable to carry out this diagnostic work and Patoss is the leading issuer of these certificates.

## Patoss Membership

Membership is open to professionals training or working in the field of SpLD. Many of our members teach in schools and colleges and many provide diagnostic assessments and one-to-one tuition to students with specific learning difficulties. We also offer supporting membership to individuals who have an interest in SpLD and wish to support the aims and activities of Patoss.

## To Find Out More

Visit the Patoss website: **www.patoss-dyslexia.org**

# The Miles Dyslexia Centre/Canolfan Dyslexia Miles, Bangor University

Marie Jones and Ann Cooke

We have changed our name this year to celebrate the work of Tim Miles, founder of our Centre and to mark his tireless efforts for dyslexic children and adults.

## Research and Development

We contributed to the standardisation of the 11–16 stage of the York Assessment of Reading Comprehension (YARC) by running the test in local secondary schools. Marie Jones has continued to represent the Centre as a member of the Working Group looking at dyslexia provision across Wales.

This year's T.R. Miles Lecture was given by Professor Charles Hulme, University of York, on The Theory and Practice of Reading Intervention.

## Student Support Service

Liz Du Pré and colleagues run the tutorial services for Bangor students in individual and group sessions, carry out screening and assessment work and provide information on dyslexia for members of staff. The service has found itself increasingly involved, within and outside the university, in promoting understanding of dyslexia and other learning differences in the workplace. A dyslexia training module for mentors/learning coaches was run again this year.

## Assessment

We offer full psychological assessment for children, students and other adults. According to what is most suitable for their needs, this can be a full EP assessment, or an assessment by a specialist teacher-assessor.

## Teaching

The teaching service is undergoing changes as there are fewer referrals from local LEAs resulting from the restructuring of their provision for dyslexic (and other) pupils with SpLD. Only the most severe cases are now referred for external specialist help. We provided sessions for the LEA INSET programme, concentrating on LSA support in KS1& 2.

We offer privately funded tuition and have a new initiative for after-school teaching. This brings in student helpers from the School of Psychology to work with pairs of children with one of our own qualified teachers.

Information and advice is also available for parents and teachers.

Wherever possible, our services are available in Welsh as well as English.

## Training Courses

The Centre runs BDA-accredited courses for qualified teachers. These are part of the School of Education part-time Diploma/ Masters programme (5 weekends run over a year). We also offer a bilingual course for LSAs.

## Teaching Resources

The latest series of reading books by Welsh members of our team are now available: Pump Penaber (The Five from Penaber), 30 magazine-style readers designed to appeal to the 10–14 age group. They follow the earlier series for younger children, Pitrwm Patrwm.

# Endnote

# Dyslexia: Keeping a Positive Mind-set

Ann Cooke

Is this a questionable statement? Some parents and teachers and dyslexic people themselves might think so. The emphasis has for so long been on the 'DYS' of DYSLEXIA: the negative aspects - problems, barriers, can'ts and general blocks against learning for those with this Specific Learning Difficulty.

A film about dyslexia was made for television in the early 70's called '8 letters beginning with D' It had substantial contributions from Tim Miles and colleagues at Bangor Department of Psychology. I have taken this as a cue for these reflections.

## How Many Words Beginning with D do People still Reel Off?

Disorder, Disadvantage, Disablement, Disorganised, even Disaster – though fortunately, nowadays not often Dumb. Tim Miles had a different attitude, which was that dyslexic children and students should think of themselves in a different way – 'Aim high. It will be hard work and it might take you longer than your friends, but you can succeed if you want to.' Unfortunately, for perhaps understandable reasons, the 'Difficulty' mind-set has become institutionalised. Parents are often Desperate to get an assessment for children who struggle with school work hoping that a Diagnosis of DYSlexia will open up the possibility of support at school. They might be given LEA and government funded individual help if they are 'bad enough'/far enough behind, Access Arrangements in exams, financial benefits for those in Higher Education in the form of computers, a book allowance and tutorial support. Dyslexic children and adults are included in DISability DIScrimination legislation which applies to education as well as to the world of employment and the public arena.

## Are We Afraid that if We Drop the DYS we Might Lose More Than We Gain?

By now, we know so much more about the causes of dyslexia and about appropriate teaching. Findings from research suggests that dyslexia is a Difference in brain organisation which makes certain ways of processing information less automatic, less easy, than for others. So should we not take a fresh stance and stop seeing it as a PROBLEM, a 'condition'. There is wide variation in the way that dyslexia shows up among individuals. But that very variability can be used to claim that it is an invention and an excuse for something else - poor teaching, poor concentration and pushy parents. It is undeniable that dyslexia brings difficulties; having to function in an educational system and a world where literacy competence is the expected norm can be a real barrier, a huge one for those more severely affected. But it is too easy to blame the 'System'. To believe that dyslexics should not be expected to read and write is unrealistic.

So how do we start altering perceptions? From experience and plenty of evidence from observations, we know that dyslexic people have talents, skills, gifts in fields where they are not constrained by having to function through reading and, especially, writing. Many inhabit a different world in which looking and doing are the modes of learning and expression. It is argued by some that these different ways of learning and doing are a *result* of dyslexia, consequent on particular brain organisation; so far there is little research that supports this view. It is more likely, the argument goes that this is a self-selective process. But this should not stop us trying see beyond the DYS, to concentrate on the CAN-DO and encourage it. If you find one channel of communication and expression difficult – in this case, literacy - then you develop alternatives which become stronger with practice. You learn to draw, paint, build, use visualisation and oral strategies, IT and so on. We know about artists, architects, engineers, designers and scientists, builders, entertainers and theatre people, car mechanics and skilled craftsmen.

These thoughts led me to a word-game. I took the word DYSLEXIA and worked through it letter by letter, writing (because I can!) all the positive expressions I could find for each one, including examples of the CAN DO's as well as more general expressions. They extended from DIFFERENCE, through IDEAS, IMAGINATIVE, to; from ARTISTIC, through APTITUDE to DRAMA, DESIGNER, INNOVATOR and LATERAL THINKER. All SUCCEEDING because they are Dyslexic, or, if you like, DESPITE Dyslexia. X was a poser. I used words beginning with EX -EXCELLENT and EXPECTATIONS – because that's how it sounds - then translated it as the symbol for KISS: love yourself and your dyslexia. This will raise self-esteem and enhance CONFIDENCE. Then I got round the X problem by using the Welsh spelling which is Dyslecsia – Welsh does not have x in its alphabet. That way, I was able to include the words CREATIVE and CELEBRATE.

Some prefer to look on dyslexia itself as a gift, one that learns and works through kinaesthetic and visual routes and emphasises meaning. So I had LEARNING STYLE: oral, kinaesthetic, doing, listening, looking. Children and adults exploring what is the best style for them and of course, to CIT. Communicating (and receiving) Information is central to Learning and Computers are Liberating and Enabling tools: word-processing, graphics, searching the web for information that can be read out, voice recognition software.

Tom West, in his book In the Mind's Eye, argues that technology is the key to the door for dyslexic people. Through that door, they are able to become successful learners, then workers and so make enormous contributions to individual and world prosperity. We neglect them at our cost. Though using computers does not suit everyone, it has often been noted that dyslexic students are particularly skilled in this respect. We should make sure that they get the best possible opportunities for learning and using technology. The drawback is that it may not be affordable for individuals when they leave education. But employers have a responsibility (through legislation under the

Disabled Persons Discrimination Acts) to provide Access for people to do their work effectively.

No-one should hide behind it but there is still a real problem for dyslexic people in that 'out there' not enough is known about the positive side. Even if individuals are accepted in the education environment, in the wider world and the workplace 'dyslexia' can still be negative and people are hesitant about admitting to it. It is up to all of us, including Dyslexic people, to shout out that the label of DYS is another way of saying DIFF: a different, distinguishable, way of being and doing. High achievers should be leading the way and many of them are happy and proud to be identified -men and women in sports, drama, TV, science and so on. Obviously only a few people will be successful to the top level; what about the rest? Nearly everyone I talk to tells me about family members and friends who are dyslexic and struggle with literacy. Many have found ways through the jungle, gained confidence in themselves by achieving in their own way. Strategies, tools, but above all, ACCEPTANCE, have helped them to come through. What do they do? All kinds of jobs and professions; they are skilled tradesmen, scientists, lawyers, artists, teachers, engineers, plumbers, police, cleaners, shop workers, soldiers and sportsmen and women. Many will say that they rely on help with writing from someone close. If they have children, they watch carefully so that they can intervene early enough to get help if it's needed.

As for LITERACY, most dyslexic people do learn to read and even to write well enough for basic purposes. But CIT could transform life for them and even the way we think about literacy. After all, the really important factor is *understanding* the content; the mechanics can be performed adequately by a machine. It should ease matters not just for those of school-age, but for people at work, or just going around everyday routines. We have all used calculators for years. Most of us now live happily with mobile phones – liberating for poor spellers. It should be no more surprising to see someone using a 'reading pen' (a hand-held scanner) or a pocketbook computer. As technology develops, the hardware gets smaller and more portable; it is also getting cheaper.

Above all, we need to work for a shift in educational policies that confine all learners to working in the same way.

So back to my game; it's something everyone can join in – at home, at school and outside it, in groups and one-to-one. Find the POSITIVE words, think UP. If a negative word is offered, turn it around, if you can, to give it a less 'down-meaning'. Encourage children, students and others to talk about the words; think about what they CAN DO. While accepting what dyslexia means to them, find ways to change negative perceptions. Help the non-dyslexic to understand and the Dyslexics to be successfully Different.

# Author Biographies

# Index of Advertisers

# Notes

# Notes